DANCING IN HEAVEN

Dancing in Heaven

Suzanne Elvidge

Published in the United Kingdom by Reconnecting Rainbows Press, 2025
ISBN 978-1-915893-14-7 (paperback edition)

Copyright © 2025 by Suzanne Elvidge

The right of Suzanne Elvidge to be identified as the author of this book has been asserted by her in accordance with the Copyright, Designs and Patents Act 1988.

Cover design by Dee Block, 2025
Photograph by Paul Armstrong / The Artistic Lens

All rights reserved. No part of this publication may be reproduced, stored in a retrieval system, or transmitted, in any form, or by any means (electronic, mechanical, photocopying, recording or otherwise) without the prior written permission of
the publisher, nor be otherwise circulated in any form of binding or cover other than that in which it is published and without a similar condition being imposed on the subsequent purchase.

Contents

Foreword		1
1	Sarah: Dancing in Heaven	3
2	Jo: Love Shack	9
3	Victoria: Doing whatever was needed	15
4	Pauline: Very nearly an armful	19
5	Erica: Touch and talking	22
6	Deborah: The heart of the Lighthouse	27
7	Laura: Tache-positive	33
8	Joan: A mother's story	36
9	Betty: Dreading Christmas	50
10	Agnes: I will not be a closet mother	56
11	Nancy: A place of safety	58
12	Emma: Long shadows	65
13	Angela: A week away at the seaside	74
14	Jenny: Icebergs and exploding mountains	77
15	Sylvia: Acting up for attention	81
16	Charlotte: The Chicken Soup Brigade	84
17	Anne: It's okay, take your time	87

18	Cathy: Listening in the silences	92
19	Cat: Near the swimming pool	96
20	Sharon: An iced bun with a cherry on top	98
21	Caro: An innocent victim	103
22	Yvonne: The best lovers are good with their hands	107
23	Hilda: It was only a little thing	113
24	Deirdre: Being a friend	115
25	Marla: Tea and whisky and striped blankets	117
26	Bridgit: Dental dams and safer sex	123
27	Pat: Excluded	125
28	Naomi: No weddings, three funerals	132
29	Audrey: We've both grown old	136
30	Kirsty: Jacob's story - it's not over yet	140

Acknowledgements   147
About the Author   148

Foreword

At many points throughout history, women's voices have been hidden, and I love finding their stories and telling them. Writing this collection has been an incredible experience – learning the inside story of Switchboard through the call logs, meeting or video calling the women who were part of the pandemic and learning stories from newspapers, magazines and websites.

These monologues sit in the blurry spaces between fact and fiction, and everyone is anonymised.

In very early 2021, as the UK was in its third national lockdown, Channel 4 aired Russell T Davies' drama series *It's a Sin*, about a group of young men living through that other viral pandemic, HIV/AIDS. It was an incredible piece of television – bitter and sweet, funny and heart-breaking. I posted on social media about how much I loved it, but that I wanted to know more about the women's voices. A friend got in touch – she had been a young nurse in the early 80s, and did I want to hear her story? Of course I did.

In March 2021, I took part in the Writing East Midlands (WEM) *Reconnecting Your LGBTQ+ Community* workshops, facilitated by Thom Seddon and Dan Webber. Through these workshops I made the nurse's story into the monologue *Dancing in Heaven*. This was later included in the WEM collection *Notes on Alone*, and Dan invited me to perform it at *Hear My Voice: a night of new writing from LGBTQ+ writers* at the Museum of Making, Derby Silk Mill.

In early 2024, Steven Atkinson (founder of the queer theatre company Roots) and writer Frazer Flintham created *Queer Spaces: Live*, a series of workshops and performances. With their help I wrote *It's okay, take your time* and performed it at the Stephen Joseph Theatre in Scarborough. Also in early 2024, I was honoured that Stephanie Fuller, the CEO of Switchboard, the national LGBTQIA+ helpline, allowed me to access the organisation's archives, including the 1980s call logs.

Chrissie Chevasutt, Outreach and Development Worker with the Transgender, Intersex and Non-binary Community at St Columba's URC saw the video from *Queer Spaces: Live!* on social media. She booked me as a headliner at the Oxford Di-Verse Poetry Festival in November 2024, where I performed *It's okay, take your time*, *Dancing in Heaven*, and *A mother's story*. There I met Ash Brockwell, a co-founder of the wonderful Reconnecting Rainbows Press, who commissioned this volume. And here we are.

One last thing – please be aware that some of these stories contain homophobic language and graphic descriptions of illness and death.

Suzanne Elvidge
1 December 2025 – World AIDS Day

1

Sarah: Dancing in Heaven

It was 1984 and I was 18 years old. My A-levels and a pre-nursing course done, I got my first job at Guy's Hospital. And so. There I was. The beginning of my new life as a nurse in a busy London hospital. I was so excited.

The placement in the infectious diseases ward brought me back down to earth with a bump.

Until then, I'd never even met anyone gay – well, not that I'd known, anyway. All I knew about that muttered word 'homosexuality' was what I saw on television or heard on the radio. Mr Humphries in *Are you Being Served*, Julian and Sandy in *Round the Horne*. Liberace. Danny La Rue. And the words whispered at my all-girls school. Shirt lifters. Benders. Poofters. All said in a way that made being gay seem like the worst thing possible. But I didn't see anything to hate.

The world was waking up to a new disease that was hitting gay men. The tabloids were shouting it, and I saw some truly awful headlines. The worst – the one that still sticks with me – was 'I'd shoot my son if he had AIDS, says vicar' in *The Sun*. I hated that paper long before Hillsborough.

The infectious diseases ward was full of men wasting away. We were given no warning, and the first time I stepped through the door, I had to clench everything not to react. Boys my age, barely out of school. Young men like my big brother. Older men who could have been my father.

At the time, all we knew was from the BBC documentary *The Killer in the Village*, and that wasn't much. Eventually they called it AIDS, but some of the nurses still called it GRID, short for 'Gay-Related Immune Disease', or ACIDS, 'Acquired Community Immunodeficiency Syndrome'. Or 4H disease, because it affected homosexuals, Haitians, heroin users and haemophiliacs. I couldn't understand why it affected those disparate groups, or what they might all have in common. I heard the older nurses whispering in corners, wondering which of the Hs the patients were. Judging them. Splitting them between the innocent victims and the guilty ones.

We had to do full barrier nursing – we were gloved and gowned and masked. The older nurses were the most afraid. So, us student nurses were sent in. Fed the patients. Washed them, talked to them. I would be lying if I said I wasn't scared. Afraid I might catch it. We didn't know anything about it – the virus hadn't got its proper name by then and it wasn't clear how it was passed on.

But I got on with it. Got to know them as real people. And their friends. Their friends were amazing! Flamboyant. So colourful in a time and place that felt like nothing but grey. They were like no-one I had ever met before. They opened my eyes to a whole new world, especially when they took me and the other young nurses to the gay club *Heaven* in Charing Cross. As well as the music and the noise and the dancing, it was the first club I'd been to where I didn't have to queue for the ladies.

We treated our patients as well as we could. But there was no cure for the virus, and it tore their immune systems and their bodies apart. Cancers. Infections. Wasting. Skin breaking down despite all our precautions. Memory loss and dementia. Tremors. I wrote letters for some of them when their shakes got too bad to be able to hold a pen.

We took it in turns sitting with distressed and dying patients, giving each other a break when we could. It was so hard to watch young men die – I remember hearing one of the more experienced nurses saying it was so much harder for them because their hearts were young and strong while their bodies were weak.

John. John, I remember so well. As the AIDS patients were in single rooms and he had few visitors, he had no one to talk to. And so, we made John laugh. The cleaner and I danced around his bed with string mop wigs on our heads and brooms as our partners. The junior doctors called in and told really bad jokes.

Our uniform was lilac and white pinstripe with a lilac collar. It was a colour that had never suited me, but I did like the short navy cape with a red lining that we wore in the hospital, and the long cloak and bonnet that kept me warm on the bleak winter walks back to the nurses' home. The bonnets made us look like we were in the Salvation Army, and an old man gave one of my friends half a crown for the Sally Anns one night. Goodness only knows how long he'd had that in his pocket.

We used to wear the short capes reversed at Christmas when we sang carols on the wards. I have to admit I got a fit of giggles when we were asked to sing *Away in the Manger* in the maternity ward.

The bit I really hated was the hats that needed a handful – no, an armful – of white hairgrips to keep them on. We had to make them up from a semicircle of starched white linen, which was stitched across the bottom with a drawstring thread to pull it into shape. The semi-circle had to be folded in these neat little pleats – either eight for the eight Beatitudes, or twelve for the twelve disciples – I can't quite remember which! We would get told off if the pleats weren't perfectly equal, and I was all fingers and thumbs. On nights when he couldn't sleep, John and I would fold a stack of them together. He showed me how to use a thin sheet of card inside to make the front stand up and keep everything tidy. He also taught me how to darn the heels of my horrible grey uniform stockings without leaving lumps that would cause blisters, and how to use soap to stop a run in my precious nylons.

I'd come from a girls' school to a hospital ward. I'd never seen a naked man before. And now I was seeing them pretty much every day. They had tattoos and piercings in places that I had no idea you could even have pierced. We had full and frank conversations,

John and me. He was so open and generous with me – a silly little girl who knew nothing.

I'd also never seen a dead person before.

I laid John out, and it was – surprising to me – a beautiful experience. Quiet and serene. It was just me and him, and it was the last gift I had to give him. I kept my cool for the rest of the day, but inside I was broken. I sobbed myself to sleep that night, and when I walked in the next day and saw his empty bed, it was all I could do not to cry. But the bed was soon filled again.

Too soon.

We had mums visiting but almost no dads. Mums who were broken. Mums who were stoic. Mums who were furious at their dying sons.

Telling John's mother that he had died was the hardest thing I had ever done. She didn't even know that he was in hospital. Like so many people at the time, he kept his sexuality and his illness a secret. So not only was I telling her that her beloved boy was gone, but I was also telling her that he was gay. I held her hand and we wept together.

We were surrounded by hate. I had people wait for me as I left hospital, asking how I could work with sinners. That God hated me for doing what I did. That AIDS cured poofs. That it was nature and the wrath of God getting rid of the aberrations. The only one that made me laugh out loud was 'God made Adam and Eve, not Adam and Steve'.

But we were also wrapped around with care. Not all parents rejected their sons. Some of them healed divisions and said goodbye with love. Some stayed on after losing their sons to befriend the boys who had lost their families. Some became activists. Some were there for us nurses, too. They brought us flasks of tea and soup and hot chocolate, and little wrapped packages of homemade biscuits and cakes. And best of all, they gave us hugs and held our hands at the end of the heart-breaking shifts.

You know what I remember most, though? Dancing in *Heaven*, sweat running down our faces, surrounded by beautiful boys in leather and lace and feathers, singing along to *Smalltown Boy* by Bronski Beat at the tops of our voices.

2

Jo: Love Shack

It came over the supermarket speakers just as I was disinterring a rock-solid bag of sweetcorn from the freezer cabinet. *Love Shack*, by the *B52s*. And suddenly I was twenty years old, exhausted, and in the role that was the hardest but best choice I had ever made.

I heard the track for the first time on the Sunday Chart Show. I was a second-year nursing student in the sluice room. In my head I can still hear the buzzy edge of the ward's tiny, tinny battery radio that I'd swiped to distract me from emptying and cleaning bed pans – not the most fun job in the world.

I was a week into a three-month placement in an AIDS and rheumatoid arthritis unit that also cared for haemophilia patients. We had learned in our lectures that haemophiliacs could bleed uncontrollably, internally and externally, even after the smallest of bumps. We were taught about the almost magical impact of the clotting factors, including Factor VIII. We were told that, while there would still be people admitted to hospitals with painful and damaged joints, it would be far fewer than ever before. What they didn't tell us – what they didn't know at the time – was that contaminated blood and blood factors from the USA were causing deaths from HIV and hepatitis infections in people with haemophilia.

When I started, I knew that there would be AIDS patients in the unit – the clue was in the name, after all – but as far as I knew, other nurses would be working with them. My focus was on the haemophilia patients. All of that changed with David. That was the day that I realised my work on the unit included end-of-life nursing, and had since the moment he arrived. And that nothing in my training could have ever prepared me for what that would actually be like.

David was the youngest of three brothers, all with haemophilia. Although in his early twenties, he was tiny, and his joints were deformed from the bleeds that had started when he began crawling at eight months old. He had soft, light brown hair in a typical schoolboy cut – I think his mum might have wielded the scissors – and a beautiful smile. Despite his enormous pain, he was so grateful for every little thing we did for him.

He wore thick glasses day and night that made his eyes look huge, and the weight of them gave him pressure sores above his ears. One day I had the bright idea to wrap oxygen tubing round the earpieces, and he loved it. He could be comfortable at last. The only slight thing was that the tubes made his ears stick right out, so that he looked like a sweet and gentle bush baby.

David's mum slept on an airbed in his en suite. I just couldn't imagine what she was going through. She'd lost one son already, she was losing another and was afraid for the third, and all we could offer was a few feet of floor in a toilet. Despite all this, she always looked beautiful – the spitting image of Honor Blackman – never a hair out of place or a smudge in her lipstick.

I never met his dad. That wasn't unusual.

One day David called me over, his face serious. He whispered to me, 'I wonder if people think I'm gay? I don't mind, but I think it might limit my chances of getting a woman!'

I wasn't sure what to say, and then he grinned, and his huge hazel eyes sparkled.

I worked nights a lot on this ward, and in the small hours of the morning I often found Dr Jameson sitting on David's bed. He was a young house officer, just a few years older than me, and I'd first met him on my previous placement on a surgical ward. I had rescued him from a nightmare spider's web of cat gut, which I rolled up in a ball and hid from the ward sister. She was a dragon over waste. Dr Jameson was always pinching the nurses' radio. He and David put it on low and listened to Radio 1, ranking the songs and disagreeing with the DJs. He taught David to play gin rummy, usually for jellybeans, and before long David had Dr Jameson in deepening layers of debt.

On those nights, when I walked past the half open door, the light splashing yellow over the polished wooden floor, they would grin and wave. I'd call in and sub Dr Jameson another bag of sweets from my apron pocket, chat for a bit and rest my feet, and then finish making my way round the sleeping ward.

I'd mentioned to Dr Jameson that I was surprised that David had a separate room, and his mother was allowed to stay, and he let slip that David had AIDS. I knew that David's older brother had died, but I hadn't been told what his cause of death had been. Looking back now, perhaps it should have been obvious, but as student nurses we weren't allowed to know which of our patients had AIDS. The unit sister said that we didn't need to know. But after David, I assumed that all my haemophilia patients had either HIV or hepatitis, or both.

The last time I saw David, just before I went off shift one morning, the radio was playing *Love Shack* and there were jellybeans all over the bed. He was wiggling his shoulders, the closest he could get to dancing. Dr Jameson was asleep in the visitors' chair, and his mum was snoring gently on her airbed. I tidied up his bed and he grinned at me, looked at his mum and Dr Jameson, and shrugged. 'Look at me,' he said. 'I'm the centre of attention!'

I walked out into the bright frosty dawn to go back to the nurses' home and sleep, the frozen leaves crunching under my feet. When I went back to the ward that night, I found out that he had died earlier in the day. Gently and quietly, his mum by his side. After that, I realised that every goodbye could be the last.

Before I went back to the classroom for my next block of teaching, I went to see the newly opened London Lighthouse along with a couple of the other nurses from the unit. They wanted us to see how people with AIDS could be cared for. The building, just off Ladbroke Grove, was beautiful, with a gleaming white lobby and rooms looking like they'd come out of the Habitat catalogue. We went to the café and talked to the staff. They told us all about the creative and complementary therapies, the medical care, the day and residential care. We sat in the communal lounge and talked to the patients. The people who worked there, from the young woman in the café to the physiotherapists, nurses and doctors were so kind, and they made life for the patients as good as possible. At that time, though, there still wasn't much they could do to stop the inexorable progress of the disease. While the first AIDS drug had been launched by then, truly effective antiretroviral therapies were still around a decade away. The gaunt, pale-faced people with AIDS looked like the walking dead, and I wept all the way home.

I moved on to a surgical ward for my next placement and it was a completely different experience. Mohamed was a refugee who had fled from Mauritania where there was a death sentence for being gay. He had been diagnosed with AIDS and he felt completely ignored by the healthcare system here in the UK. He was so desperate to get medical care he swallowed bleach, which burned holes in his oesophagus. The porters were so scared of being near him they just rammed his bed into the door and fled in panic. Mohamed's chest drain bottle crashed to the floor and shattered, scattering glass and body fluids everywhere. The room stank of blood and infection, and he sobbed in pain and fear. I shouted for someone to get the biohazard crew in to clear it all up, and I did my best to comfort the shaking young man. He was treated with such gentleness and care by everyone, even when he had to have treatment that was so toxic we needed to wear full protective clothing, including masks. Just like David, he was so brave, so tolerant, so grateful.

At the time I was furious with the porters, but now I think about it, they knew even less about the disease than we did at that point, and were so poorly paid they couldn't afford to be ill. If I'm going to blame anyone, it should be the people who created those horrific adverts and leaflets. If you weren't already afraid and confused before you saw them, you certainly would be after.

It wasn't just the porters who were afraid. I've worked with nurses who would avoid going near the AIDS patients if they could help it, or just mutter under their breath about how they only got what they deserved. But I also worked with nurses who were grace in human form – they would sit on the beds and hold the patients' hands. Talk to them into the night. Comfort their families. And then weep quietly in the sluice room.

And I still can't listen to *Love Shack*, even now.

I dropped the veg back into the freezer and walked out, leaving a bemused shop floor worker staring at my half-full trolley.

We can always have beans on toast for tea.

3

Victoria: Doing whatever was needed

Back in the 80s, when you worked in the lab in a rural hospital, you did whatever was needed. Especially at the weekend, and even more especially when it looked like something was very wrong. That Saturday, I'd done the cross-matching for a blood transfusion and sorted out a patient's anticoagulant levels when a nurse dropped off a urine sample on her way past. Once I'd deciphered the consultant's handwriting – you get good at that after a while – I realised that the patient was dreadfully underweight and really ill. It sounded like tuberculosis, and I knew that it wouldn't wait until Monday.

I walked through to the silent and empty microbiology lab and looked at the sample under the microscope. I expected to see *Mycobacterium tuberculosis* and saw nothing but *Salmonella,* which is usually in the gut – you remember all the fuss about eggs and Edwina Currie, don't you? I was sure it wasn't a contaminant but, just in case, I cleaned the bench down again – the alcohol fumes always made my eyes sting – and dug out a fresh lab coat and horrible latex gloves. A nurse dashed round with a stool and urine sample from the patient. Some nurses get all the best jobs. As do some lab technicians.

Nothing in the stool and still just *Salmonella* in the urine. Not like anything I'd ever seen before.

I rang the results back to the ward, left a note on my boss's desk and went home, chalking it up to a medical mystery that my team could untangle on Monday.

Monday lunchtime, my boss called to ask if I would come into the lab. I was off after the weekend, but he sounded worried. Unlike his usual calm self. So, I went in.

He said he'd been on the phone to other labs all morning and they had seen what I'd seen. His face was grave. He said it looked like it was all part of an outbreak that was happening worldwide and looked like it was escalating. It didn't even have a proper name or a cause yet, but he thought it was probably going to be bloodborne. And he thought it would most likely be bad. But between us, we had no idea how bad it was actually going to be.

Even though we didn't know the full story yet, my boss and I decided that I should put measures in place to protect the team, but as far as possible not to scare them. As the news about what would come to be called HIV spread, people got more anxious about handling blood and other body fluids, and I lost some really great members of staff. One because he was afraid of people finding out that he was gay, another because her husband wanted her out of the lab and made her life ever more difficult until she resigned.

Even though there was so much fear swirling around in the media, not everyone seemed to get it. I felt I was educating people all the time, even the doctors, who I really thought should know better. They assumed that because it was a 'gay plague', it had nothing to do with them and their nice, clean patients.

At the time, blood and body fluid samples weren't routinely put in plastic bags like they are now, and I was constantly telling doctors that they needed to do it to protect their staff and mine. I thought that at least the people in the labs would take things on board, but apparently not. One woman I worked with hated wearing gloves and took them off every time she tested samples from an antenatal clinic. According to her, there was no risk because they were healthy young women, not gay men. I couldn't believe it. Not only were the press and media scapegoating gay men, but my colleagues were doing it too.

I asked her, 'What is the one thing you know about them?'

She didn't reply.

I told her, 'They are pregnant, and that happens after people have sex. Sex is how this is spread. And before you say anything – yes, that includes men and women having sex. So, we have to treat every sample as if it contains this mystery infection.'

She went really quiet, but she did put her gloves on. And a couple of days later, I overheard her telling one of the trainees to put his gloves on, 'because even pregnant women might have infections'.

I was so proud of her. She was doing whatever was needed.

4

Pauline: Very nearly an armful

Every time I give blood, I'll hear someone, somewhere say, 'It may be just a smear to you, mate, but that's life and death to some poor wretch,' or 'A pint! That's very nearly an armful!' I admire the nurses who smile, and my heart goes out to the ones who've heard it seventeen times that morning and who are trying to stop an almost audible eye roll.

Tony Hancock made *The Blood Donor* in 1961, but somehow those two quotes just never seem to fade away. A bit like a blood stain on a favourite white shirt - but that's a whole different story.

My dad took me along to blood donor sessions when I was little so I wouldn't be scared, and I sat in the 'resting with a cup of tea' area, being fed biscuits and weak orange squash by doting nurses. I started giving blood when I was 18, and got even more passionate about it when I started working for the National Blood Service in the 1970s. I've given over a hundred donations so far, and I'm going to keep going as long as I can, even if they have to wheel me in!

The blood donation service must keep a balance. We must make sure that donated blood is as safe as possible, because patients who need a transfusion are already seriously ill. But we have to keep donors on our side as well, as they generously give their time as well as their blood.

This balance got harder as the AIDS crisis evolved.

I remember the first time we heard that there was an illness spreading that was damaging the immune system in gay men. There was no test then – in fact, then we didn't even know whether it was a virus or not – but we knew we needed to be careful. It felt as if we were fumbling about in the dark. As the disease was affecting mostly young gay men, we figured that it was probably passed on through the semen. And if it was in semen – well, it was pretty safe to assume that it could be in other body fluids too, including blood. While we hated doing it, we decided that we had to ask male donors whether they were in a sexual relationship with a man, and if so, we had to turn them away. It was horrible for us and for them.

When anyone made their first donation, we would do a whole raft of tests, including checking whether the donor was well enough to donate, and then each time we had to check if anything had changed since the last one.

We started testing for hepatitis B and a couple of other infections. These together were what are called surrogate tests. While they weren't perfect, when people we thought might be at risk tested positive for two out of three, we didn't use their blood. However, the word got out that the blood service had a test, which meant that more high-risk people came forward, seemingly to donate but really so that they could get some kind of a check-up. You can't blame them – these were scary and desperate times, especially for gay men who had a partner who was ill or had died.

When we finally got hold of a specific HIV test, we were able to use it before it was available to doctors. We kept it quiet though – while it seemed unfair, we didn't want to risk another wave of people coming forward just to get a test result. We wouldn't be able to cope with the demand. We also didn't want to risk infected blood getting into the system, especially as blood donations can be split into different products, so one affected donation could end up infecting a slew of different people.

The blood stain on my favourite shirt? That was when I was drafted in to teach doctors to take blood samples. One particularly heavy-handed student made such a mess of it that I ended up with what looked like an entire roll of bandage round my arm and a promise of dinners for a week if I didn't tell his supervisor. I've still got the scar. We went out for a few months before he realised that I wasn't his type, in more ways than one. We're still friends now and his husband, who is a nurse, tells the story to everyone who will listen.

The moral of the story? Always get a nurse to take your blood – not a surgeon in training!

5

Erica: Touch and talking

I first got involved in the Lighthouse project in the early months of 1986. Paul – my only sibling – had died of AIDS. I'd looked after him in those awful last weeks and months. I watched him turn from my funny, beautiful, blond big brother, gay in so many senses of the word, to a shuffling and stooped husk of a man, ancient in his thirties.

I was emerging from that early, raw numbness of grief when all I had wanted to do was hibernate, and I needed a really good reason to leave the house. Then it arrived – a letter from one of Paul's friends asking me if I'd like to come along to a meeting. They were talking about how we could better look after people who were HIV-positive, or those who had what we used to call AIDS-related complex and full-blown AIDS. When I looked after Paul, I saw how stretched the hospitals and staff were, and how beds for urgent medical care were filled by people who needed support but didn't necessarily need to be in hospital. At the time I knew there had to be another way to do it, but I didn't have room in my head to work out what that way was, or how it could be done.

The small meeting room was full of voices bouncing excitedly over each other, talking about how to look after people in the community rather than in a hospital. Creating a place where people with AIDS could get counselling, friendship, even just a cup of coffee in a safe space. Somewhere they could source the help they needed at home. And then, when things got harder, somewhere they could convalesce, or go to for terminal care, however long or short a time that might be. Somewhere they could live better and die well.

And that's how London Lighthouse was born.

I volunteered to help with raising funds. This project was going to cost a lot of money. But that wasn't the only decision I made that night. I'd got talking to a couple of people with AIDS, and they told me what difference a physiotherapist had made to them. I'd taken a break from working in a bank to look after Paul, and I had been thinking about doing something different with my life. Perhaps physiotherapy was the something different I could do.

The Borough Road College campus in Osterley, part of the West London Institute of Higher Education, was happy to take me and my two A levels. The determined staff set about taking a classful of school leavers and career changers and turning us into physiotherapists. After many lectures, some very long days working as nurse assistants, which taught us how hospitals actually worked, and a thousand hours of clinical placements during the holidays, we were launched onto an unsuspecting world. Wearing brand new uniforms and clutching dog-eared textbooks like comfort blankets.

Studying had kept me busier than I had ever imagined, but I still managed to keep in touch with the London Lighthouse team. I shook buckets, sent letters and watched the derelict school in Notting Hill turn from a building site to a thing of beauty.

I was working in a hospital in Birmingham when, a few months after the Lighthouse opened, I got a letter offering me a job. I yelled so loudly my next-door neighbour in the nurses' home came rushing round, convinced I'd hurt myself. Then she yelled loudly too – it turned out that she had trained as a nurse with a man who had developed AIDS. He'd written to her about the therapy he'd received at the London Lighthouse, and how much the care there had meant to all the patients whose families wouldn't touch them or talk to them.

On my first day, they gave me a tour of the amazing building that I'd last seen full of workmen and ladders. The beautiful colours. The light and bright hallways. The staff wearing their own clothes, not starched uniforms. Communal areas filled with people working, talking, laughing, reading. The single and shared rooms where the residents – not patients – could stay for convalescence, respite or palliative care. It was somewhere that death was a part of life, in a real way, not a head on one side and gentle voice kind of way.

As soon as I walked onto the unit at the beginning of a shift, I always checked the board where the residents' names and room numbers were chalked up. Picking out the names that were the same and the ones that had changed. The ones that weren't there. Some I knew had gone home. And some hadn't. That's just how it was.

Art was a doctor, a surgeon, and he had a stack of British Medical Journals on the table next to his bed. He kept me up to date on the latest research as I worked on his hands, and I passed any useful nuggets onto the others in the team. Nerve damage meant that he had lost feeling in his fingers. He knew he wasn't going to be able to go back to work as a surgeon, but he planned to teach. His secretary, the only one of his colleagues who came to visit, would take dictation in the evening and every piece he had published in journals and magazines would be pinned up in the nurses' station.

George was with us for convalescence. He'd been in intensive care with a bad bout of pneumonia, and my job was to help him get him moving again. He always made a fuss about the exercise when his friends were visiting and they were sharing a bottle of wine, but he was good as gold when it was just the two of us.

Simon was there for palliative care. We talked together about what I was doing to prevent his joints from getting stiffer than they already were. He knew his disease as well or better than I did, and like with all the other residents, we made decisions together – that felt really important. All the time we worked together the room was filled with the hissing sound of the air blowing through the silica sand in his bed. This reduced his risk of pressure sores, because as he got more ill his skin became so delicate.

Simon got me to make a list of names and addresses of his friends so that his family could contact them after he died. Each time I left him, I had to promise to come to his funeral if he passed away before my next visit. He told me that he would haunt me if

I didn't. I told him I would exorcise him if he did - and yes, of course, I would be there.

When he died, a month after we first met, I didn't cry. I just got on with things, despite the fact that he had become my friend as well as my patient. But when a patient I had only known for 24 hours died a few weeks later, I broke down. Delayed grief, I suppose. Two of the nurses swept me up and took me down to the café. The sweet young woman who worked there brought me hot chocolate and cheesecake, and the nurses held my hands until I got calmer. They knew that I would do the same for them, and for all the other people who worked at the London Lighthouse.

Touch and talking wasn't just my job.

It was how we all kept going.

6

Deborah: The heart of the Lighthouse

The café always felt like the heart of the London Lighthouse.

I saw the job on a postcard in the Job Centre. I'd left school, and my sister was trying to get me to work with her at Alice's Antiques on Portobello Road, but I didn't really want to be around all that old stuff. Or even around my sister. I mean, she's great. But all day, every day?

I had no idea what the London Lighthouse was, but the lady at the Job Centre explained it to me. I wasn't really sure about it at first and I talked to my mum and dad. My mum wasn't keen, but my dad said that I should try it for a bit – it was only a café, and I wouldn't have to see any of the patients, after all – it would just be the people who worked there. I think Dad and I thought it was going to be the staff canteen. We were both wrong, but I soon fell in love with the place and the people.

I started a week before the building opened in September 1988, so that I could help the café manager set it all up. Organise the cupboards and fill the sugar bowls, all those sorts of things. They showed me everything, from the residential unit with its single and shared rooms, to the hall that would become the hub for meetings, conferences and even funerals. Everywhere was bright and clean, full of beautiful colours and glass walls. It was the lightest place I'd ever seen. Everyone made me feel so welcome, even though I was only a school leaver who was going to work in the café, but they told me that I was just as important as anyone else.

My manager in the café was friends with some of the people who had been there from the beginning, and he was really excited about the whole project. He talked about his brother who had died from AIDS, and I told him that I'd never met anyone gay. He smiled and told me that I had, that morning. I looked round and he laughed. 'It's me,' he said. I'm really embarrassed when I think about it now, but I said, 'You can't be. You look normal!' I was only sixteen then.

He hugged me and told me not to worry – that I was going to meet all kinds of different people while I worked there. We talked about the café and what it was for – that it wasn't just for the staff, it was for the residents who were staying at the unit, and for their patients and families. It was also for people who were there for counselling, art therapy and support groups, or just wanted to meet friends for coffee, cakes and a game of Monopoly. He said that I could bring my family and friends on my day off, if I wasn't already bored of the place. I said I would, but I wasn't ever going to play Monopoly again with my sister. I'd learned my lesson at Christmas. He laughed.

I did meet all kinds of people and hear all kinds of stories. I have to admit it took me a while at first to get used to seeing some of the residents, but before too long it all felt – well, not normal, but ordinary.

One day, one of the residents said he felt like everyone he knew was afraid of him. Can you imagine feeling like that? I told him I was afraid of dogs, but I wasn't afraid of him, and he gave me a beautiful, tired smile. I patted his shoulder as I walked away, and he started to cry. I ran over to one of the physiotherapists who I'd got to know – I think she was my manager's friend – and she sat with him. I asked her afterwards what I'd done wrong, and she said that I hadn't done anything wrong, he just couldn't remember the last time someone had touched him like that. After that, I patted his shoulder every time I saw him in the café. If we were in the corridors, he would bob down so I could pat his shoulder (he was very tall, and I am very short!)

Another day, when I was clearing the tables, a nurse and I were talking about the stories that were appearing in the papers about the London Lighthouse, and she told me that she got anxious every time there were people from the press here, as she didn't want her picture in the news. That surprised me at first – I mean, who doesn't want their picture taken? But she explained that she doesn't want her family and her flatmate to know that she works with AIDS patients, because of what they will say. I hadn't even thought of that. She said it's the same for some of the residents or the people coming to clinics, because their families don't even know that they are gay, let alone HIV-positive.

We had some long, hard days when favourite residents died or when people protested outside, shouting awful things. One day a friend of my manager, a big guy who went to the gym every day, escorted us out and made sure we got home okay. My mum didn't want me to go back again but I told her I had to. I couldn't let anyone down. My dad gave me a big hug and told me he was proud of me.

We all looked after each other.

We had some exciting days too. Elizabeth Taylor visited, and she was so beautiful. She smiled at me. I couldn't wait to tell my mum – we loved watching Elizabeth Taylor films like *National Velvet* and *Cat on a Hot Tin Roof* on a Sunday afternoon. And *Cleopatra* with Richard Burton. He was so handsome.

We sometimes saw Ian McKellen. Apparently, he'd had a friend who died of AIDS, and so he put on a one-man show called *Acting Shakespeare* that raised enough money for them to start work on the London Lighthouse. The hall is named after him. I never understood Shakespeare, but Mr McKellen was a lovely man.

The Pink Singers choir came along one day in their gorgeous pink shirts and bow ties and made us all laugh. They performed on the roof of Broadcasting House too, which just sounded a bit scary to me.

There was the official opening in November 1988, with Princess Margaret. She was so beautiful and wore such a lovely blue dress. She unveiled a plaque, and they played *That's What Friends are For* by Stevie Wonder. That became a bit of a theme tune for all our events. She was our Patron, and I think having people like her come to see us made the public less scared.

Princess Margaret also used to visit here secretly with her friend Anne Glenconner, when Anne's son was a resident. There was no fuss at all, just two friends visiting. No photographs or anything. One of the cleaners said she saw Princess Margaret give Henry, Anne's son, a big hug, just like it was an ordinary day. The cleaner also said that Princess Margaret made the men laugh, and loved that it made them sound like they could forget why they were all there, just for a moment. I heard that the princess went to Henry's funeral. That was so kind of her. She must have liked Anne a lot – apparently, they had known each other since they were little.

The whole place smelled of paint the day Princess Diana visited, in 1989. I didn't get to see her, apart from a glimpse of her car through the window, but the café was full of laughter afterwards, like it was a wedding reception or something. She'd hugged and shaken hands with people with AIDS. That meant a lot to all of us, but most of all, I will always remember Princess Margaret slipping in and out so quietly to see Henry.

There was an auction of artworks for London Lighthouse, and I got to go along to help out behind the scenes at Christie's – that's a big auction place, you know. I took drinks around to beautifully dressed people and got to see all the pictures. I didn't like all of them – there was a huge painting of a very pink naked woman being held by what I think was supposed to be a statue, and another painting of a wonky kitchen chair by a blond man with big black glasses. Some of the smaller pictures were really lovely, though.

Proper pictures that I would have on my wall. Not that I would ever have been able to afford any of them. Not in a million years. One of the people working at Christie's kindly gave me a catalogue at the end of the evening, when they saw me looking. I've still got it on my shelf.

I'm not an angel. I had days that my feet hurt, I hated my job, and I couldn't get the smell of veggie chilli out of my hair, however many times I washed it. Days when I'd been told off by my boss for nipping out for one cigarette too many and I sulked for an hour. Or when I'd had to count to seventeen not to snap at the doctor who came in for a cup of tea, ten minutes after I'd closed up and switched everything off. But there really weren't many of those days, and even on the worst ones I remembered what this place does and why it was here. And yes, of course I forgave the doctor and made her a cup of tea with a biscuit from my private stash.

7

Laura: Tache-positive

I heard him shouting across to his dental nurse, even before I opened the door. He had a voice that could cut across oceans let alone low-budget plywood doors.

'Got another tache-positive tonight.'

Well, that's a start to a Monday, I thought to myself.

What he meant was we had an HIV-positive patient coming in. If it happened today, I would say something. But then, I was an overawed and anxious dental student trying to please everyone.

As dentists, we could be the first to see that there was something wrong. Sometimes before the patient knew, or wanted to admit it. I had a tutor at college who said that the mouth tells the story, and that summer I realised how right he was. Warts. White hairy patches on the tongue. Thrush. Ulcers. Gum disease. The swelling on the roof of the mouth that could be a sign of Kaposi's sarcoma. Things I'd only ever seen in textbooks. I had to learn not to look surprised.

If we knew beforehand that a patient was HIV-positive, it was all the precautions. Appointments at the end of the day. Sending all but essential staff home. Wearing plastic disposable gowns, mask and glasses, and two sets of gloves. And then everything in the bin before we went home. That August was airless and endless, and I knew I would be soaked with sweat even before the patient arrived.

The clock ticked round to five-thirty, and a young man walked into the empty waiting room. His name was Keith. Tall and good-looking. Lean to the point of thinness. He wore tight jeans and a white shirt and the sweat patches under his arms showed how nervous he was, especially when he saw me wrapped up from head to toe, beckoning him through. I pulled my mask down and grinned at him and I got a tiny tight smile back. My boss – well – he just looked at the young man over his glasses and I tensed, waiting for his comment.

'Nice moustache,' he said.

Keith looked confused and the nurse rolled her eyes. I mouthed an apology and then pulled my mask back up as my boss glared at me.

Keith lay waiting, dwarfed by the plastic-shrouded dental chair. What surprised me was, whatever he said, how gentle my boss was as he worked on Keith's damaged and broken mouth. I almost changed my views on him, until I heard him mutter about fairies as the door shut. Thankfully this time it was so quiet only I heard.

Now, when I teach my students about the role of dentists in diagnosing systemic illness, from kidney disease to blood cancers, I tell them about that young man. About how I would be paid a fiver a time to test out anti-fungal mouth washes and toothpastes. And about how great professionals can be complex people. But no names, no pack drill.

After all, they might recognise my boss's name as the author of the textbook I recommend. The best book I've read on oral disease in HIV.

8

Joan: A mother's story

1962

He was such a beautiful baby. The most beautiful baby I'd ever seen. I know every mum and grandma says that, but I really think he was.

I'd waited such a long time for him. Every month I held my breath, and then the curse would arrive. I saw the doctor, who said that we should relax and just let nature take its course. I blamed myself. I blamed Tom. We had all the tests, and the doctor told us that it was no-one's fault. Sometimes it just happened.

I said we should ask for prayers at church. Tom hated the idea, but he did it for me. And... nothing.

They said that it was God's will. Tom and I decided just to get on with our lives, and they were good lives. But every baptism and every sympathetic smile at church made my heart ache. I just had to remember. God was on my side.

My monthlies stopped. I thought it was the menopause, which came early in my family. To be honest, I was relieved to say goodbye to them – every pack of Dr Whites was a reminder of my failure. But it didn't feel like the description of the menopause in the Family Medical Guide. I was tired, right down to my bones, I lost my appetite, and my mouth – I can't quite describe it – my mouth tasted off.

Tom sent me to the doctor, who said it sounded like a virus and asked for a urine sample. I didn't give it a second thought, so when I got the phone call two weeks later – well, you can imagine. All my dreams, all my prayers had come true. God is love.

It wasn't an easy pregnancy. They often aren't when you are older, but Tom and the church supported me every step of the way. And in hospital, surrounded by cards and gifts and bouquets, I watched his tiny perfect face unfolding like a flower and that made it all worthwhile. Being a first-time mother at 43 – my notes called me an ' elderly primigravida' – wasn't exactly easy, but we muddled through with love and tiredness and tears and joy.

1978

Paul was an easy boy. No trouble at all. Sang in the choir and went to youth group at church, led Sunday School, did well in his exams. Everything I'd ever hoped for.

Tom took him to football, and I took him to drama classes, and to the cinema. We went to see Derek Jarman's *The Tempest* because he was studying that for A level, and to a David Hockney exhibition for his art studies.

He was popular, good looking, clever, kind. He wasn't perfect – the damage he did when he first discovered scissors at three years old would make your hair curl – but he was as close as I could ever want.

Our village was small and quiet, so I wasn't really surprised when the social life wasn't enough for him. He used to catch the bus into town with his friends from the drama group. They were a nice lot. A bit flamboyant and political for me, but they looked out for each other, and I suppose I thought that Paul would be the calming influence. Colin was his best friend, and they did everything together. Colin even started to come to church with us and I was thrilled. I saw a few people giving Colin funny looks – I think it was the long hair and the earring – but I didn't care. God was for everyone. God is love, after all.

Paul came home drunk a couple of times when he was out with Colin and his other drama group friends. I didn't like it, but Tom persuaded me to let it go. That it was just a phase. I prayed about it, and it didn't happen again.

God continued to be on our side.

1980

Paul was the first of our family to go to university, and I guess I'd hoped he might want to study English or something like that not too far away. But he decided that he wanted to go to drama school in London.

Things started to change after he went away. I was so looking forward to him coming home for weekends, but we didn't see him until Christmas. When he was growing up, we talked about anything, everything, but now he seemed... further away. I asked him about his course, his flatmates, whether he'd met any nice girls. Whether he had settled into a church. What plays he was doing. He said they'd been studying *The Boys in the Band*, and I asked if he'd enjoyed it. He smiled an odd little smile. He was polite, but just not the chatty little boy I knew before. He spent a lot of the holiday with Colin and even slept over at his house a couple of times. I couldn't understand why – Colin was only a few streets away – but Paul said that they were staying up late listening to music and didn't want to disturb us.

Colin hadn't gone away to university, and I found out that he had been up to London to stay with Paul a few times during the autumn term. I said that if Colin had told us, we could have driven over together. He smiled another odd little smile and changed the subject.

I didn't understand. Didn't he want to see us? I wept on Tom's shoulder. Tom persuaded me to let it go. That it was just a phase.

I hated Paul going back to drama school after Christmas, but in an odd way it was almost a relief.

I prayed about it.

I knew that God would always be on our side.

1981

The phone rang one evening. I'd fallen asleep on the sofa and Tom was watching the Nine O'Clock News. It was talking about patients in America dying of a strange kind of pneumonia. I said I'd go and wondered who it was. Nobody we knew rang after 8 in the evening. It was Paul – I could tell by the sound of the coin in the call box – and I asked if I could call him back. He said it was okay; he had a stack of 10p pieces. I settled down on the telephone table's padded seat for a chat.

His voice was strained. He said he had something to say, and that I might be angry. I told him I could never be angry with him.

There was a pause, and my mouth went dry. Was he ill or something? Or had he failed his course?

He cleared his throat and said 'Mum, I'm gay.'

I couldn't take it in at first.

He said, 'Did you hear me, Mum? I'm *gay* – a homosexual. Colin is my boyfriend.'

I dropped the phone. I couldn't speak. Move. Perhaps I cried out. I don't know.

Tom came rushing in and asked whatever was wrong. He picked up the phone from the floor and spoke to Paul. I have no idea what they actually said. All I heard was voices and the ding as the phone went down.

Tom held me as I sobbed. He told me that it was probably just another phase.

I told him I was going to ring Paul back. Talk to him. Speak the truth in love. Tom said not to. To wait until I was calmer. But actually, I was perfectly calm.

I dialled and Paul picked up. He must have been standing right next to the phone. I asked him what I had done wrong that he turned out this way. I blamed his drama friends. I explained as calmly as I could that he was making a choice that went against God's law. That he was involving himself in sexual practices that the Bible said are sinful.

There was another silence. Paul said 'Mum, I'm sorry. This isn't a choice. This is who I am. I love Colin. I hope that you can still love me.'

I said of course I did – that I could love the sinner and still hate the sin.

He quietly said that he didn't – couldn't – think it was a sin. That if God really did create him, he created him as a gay man.

I said I just couldn't agree, but I offered to send him some leaflets so that he would understand. I said I would come to the college with our pastor and pray with him. Pray that he would be healed.

There was a silence. The longest so far.

He told me again that this was who he was and how he was made and that he didn't need healing. And again, he said that he hoped I could still love him.

I closed my eyes and prayed.

He asked if I was still there.

I said that I was. But I couldn't condone what he had chosen to be, and that he was going to have to choose between being a homosexual and being with us and God.

He laughed. It was a bitter, small laugh. And he said that in that case, it seemed that both God and I had abandoned him. He put the phone down on me. Me. His mother.

Tom didn't speak to me for the rest of the evening. Or the next week. But I knew that God was on my side. God disciplines those he loves, and we as parents have to love and discipline our children in the same way.

I kept praying. I mean – it wasn't Paul. I knew *he* wasn't gay. It must be that Colin and the other students. Paul always wanted to please other people, and perhaps he thought that he could only be friends with them if he said that he was gay.

I sent him tracts, magazines, books given to me by people at church. After a while they started to be returned unopened. My heart broke. I cried every day. I realised that I was grieving for my son as if he was dead. Which he was, to me, anyway.

Tom didn't understand how I could treat our son like this. He couldn't see that this was for Paul's own good. Tom stopped coming to church, but the church stayed there for me. They became my family. They reassured me that God was on my side. That I was allowed to hate the sin that Paul was committing. That they knew I loved Paul, and that God loved me.

The summer of 1984

Tom was out. Again. He'd been out a lot lately. He didn't say where, and I didn't ask. The copy of *Eros Defiled* I left by Tom's bedside lay unread, yellowed and curled.

We lived together like wary flatmates these days, fine provided we didn't talk about God or Paul. My friends at church were my haven – the place I could really talk. They understood what it was like, and they prayed for me. For us.

At church, the pastor introduced me to a woman called Sheila – he said that her son was also under the delusion that he was gay. I think he thought that she would be my comfort. I liked her. I could talk to her, and she listened, but I felt like she was holding something back. One day over coffee she gave me some books. One was called *Jonathan Loved David,* and another was called *Is the Homosexual my Neighbour?*

I started to read them, but I didn't understand why she had given them to me. It was almost as if she didn't see anything wrong with her son being gay. That she thought God was fine with it.

I told the pastor about them. He told me to burn them, and that if I had the Bible I didn't need those other books. God wasn't on her side.

I never saw Sheila again at church. But I kept the books.

Late 1984

Tom had been away in London on business for a couple of weeks, and he came home, his face grey.

In the hall, the Daily Mail lay on the doormat – *AIDS Virus Kills Man in Britain.*

He said he'd kept in touch with Paul. That they'd been meeting up when he said that he was away for work. This time when he arrived at Paul and Colin's flat, the neighbour said that they weren't there, and there had been an ambulance. I felt the room swim.

Tom told me that when he arrived at the hospital, Colin said that Paul had what they called AIDS. That he was dying.

I told him I wanted to see Paul, but Tom's face told me it was too late.

Had I hated the sin so much that I had forgotten about the love?

1985

I told people at church that Paul had died of cancer, which he had, in a way. When the news got out that it was AIDS, they still welcomed me, but they no longer mentioned Paul. It was as if he had never existed.

Tom gave me details of a grief group for people who had lost someone because of AIDS. He'd seen a counsellor through work, and he said it had really helped. I brushed it off. I had my church and my God.

He kept mentioning it. I still didn't want to go, but in the end I agreed because I thought it might please him. And stop him going on about it, too.

Tom dropped me off. It was a damp spring day, and the hall was cold and dim. There were chairs huddled in a circle in the middle of the room, and groups of people standing about talking, mostly young men but a couple of older women too. The walls were hung with crepe paper daffodils, limply celebrating Mother's Day. I felt so out of place. So alone. I turned to leave – it was just too much – and a gentle hand stopped me. A tall greying man, thin and slightly stooping, led me to a chair. Someone – I didn't see who – brought me a cup of tea.

The older man called everyone to sit down and asked us to introduce ourselves. I kept silent. I didn't want to be there, and it was all I could do not to run. It started with a few of the young men talking about their boyfriends. Their lovers. The friends they had lost. The funerals they'd been to.

The anger started to bubble up inside of me. As yet another young man started to talk about his so-called partner, I couldn't hold it in anymore. I stood up and shouted: 'You might have lost the people you call your lovers, but I lost my son!' It wasn't like me. I don't do things like that, but the years of pain and loss just had to get out.

'It's all of your faults – you and people like you. If he hadn't met people like you. If he hadn't done what people like you do. If he hadn't been gay, he'd still be alive.'

The room fell silent around me. No-one moved, until the young man opposite stood up.

He spoke quietly. He said that his name was John. And his grief for his boyfriend Dave was as great as mine was for my son.

The anger in my chest went from red to white hot. I couldn't speak. How dare he suggest that a mother's loss is no greater than that of any supposed 'boyfriend'? One of the women held out her hand to me, but I ran out of the door, straight into Tom. He'd been waiting for me. I think he'd expected me to run away.

We drove home in silence, and then when we got in I started to rant. He listened, and when I finally ran out of steam, he looked me in the eye and asked me how I would feel if *he* died.

I told him that was different – that we were married. That we'd been married for forty years.

He then asked me how I would have felt if he hadn't come home from the army – if he'd been killed before we even had the chance to marry. If I'd been John and he'd been Dave.

I nearly choked on my tea. It wasn't the same.

He asked me how it wasn't the same. And I didn't answer. Wouldn't answer. Couldn't make myself answer. I just mumbled that it was different.

He said he was going for a walk, to leave me to think. I sat there for what seemed like hours.

I could no longer see any love. And I wasn't sure whether I could see God anymore.

1986

Tom left a week later. He said he couldn't live with me feeling as I did.

It took over a year, but we finally sold the house. When I unpacked my things in the garden flat that half the money had allowed me to buy, I found the books that Sheila had given me. I thought I'd thrown them away. I'm not quite sure why I started reading them, but I read them from cover to cover. Sheila's phone number was there on the first page, and I rang it, not knowing how she would react, or even if she was still there.

She was. And she was so kind. She'd been wanting to contact me but didn't know how.

We met up and talked for hours. She had found a new church that embraced her and her son. He had a partner and fortunately they were both fit and well. She introduced me to the vicar, and we talked a lot about my views and his, and about what the books had said. I grieved for Paul and for my broken relationship with him and with Tom, and how much hurt I had caused. And Sheila and the vicar together persuaded me to go back to the grief group.

I told them I would think about it. I also told them that I was starting to feel, not that God was on my side, but perhaps I was moving back to being on God's side.

1987

Two and a half years after Paul's death and two years almost to the day that I'd stormed out, I walked into the cold dim hall again. The tall greying man, a little greyer now, was putting the chairs out. He looked at me warily and I smiled. Apologised. Explained.

I kept quiet the first few weeks, listening, and then, haltingly, I told my story. I told them that I'd lost Paul twice, when I sent him away and when he died. I told them that I was sorry.

I stayed at that group until the end of the crisis. I felt like the young men there became my sons in some kind of way. Of course, they didn't replace Paul. They couldn't ever do that. But I loved them. And while I don't dare speak for the Almighty, I now understand that love is love.

9

Betty: Dreading Christmas

I'm already dreading Christmas and it's only June.

They found Andrew in his chair next to the window in his bedsit, the one with the view of the sea. That was his favourite spot, where he could see the bird feeders hanging off the fire escape. The window was open to the spring breeze. The phone handset was hanging off, and there was a pill bottle on his lap.

I'd insisted that he have a phone put in. When he said that it would be too expensive, I told him I had a bit saved up from the housekeeping, and that his dad didn't need to know. I just wanted to know that he could get hold of me if he needed to, without having to wait for the pay phone in the hall or walk down to the call box at the end of the road.

I will always wonder who he was talking to at the end. I hope they were kind.

Andrew's dad was old-fashioned. Straightforward. Ken called a spade a spade and all that. At work all week, with dinner on the table when he got home. Weekends doing DIY, gardening and washing the car. A fortnight's holiday every year in 'works weeks', in the same seaside town that he'd been to every year growing up.

When Andrew came along, Ken was thrilled. I gave up my job. These days, they call it being a stay-at-home mum, but then it was just what many of us did.

I needed this kind of ordinary life, growing up as a latchkey kid from a broken home. I was the daughter of a single mother before that was even a thing. Lots of love, but lots of loneliness .and often being hungry.

Andrew told me that he was gay when he was seventeen. I didn't see it coming. I mean – he hadn't talked about girlfriends, but I'd just thought that perhaps he was shy. And he didn't seem – well, he didn't seem gay. I know now that not everyone does, but then, all you ever saw was limp wrists and *Are You Being Served*. It was a different time. A different world.

The first thing he said – well, the second, after saying he was gay – was not to tell his dad. Because he knew that it wouldn't go down well.

I kept Andrew's secret for him.

Andrew was an easy-going kid. Ken always wanted Andrew to study to be an engineer at the local poly on day release and follow him to the works. He pushed him into studying the sciences, but

Andrew rebelled – probably the first time he ever had – and got a place at Brighton Polytechnic to train to be an infant teacher. Ken couldn't understand why a man would want to teach young children, because that was a job for women. And that he hoped people didn't think that Andrew was a poof, or someone who liked children rather too much – because they were the same thing, anyway.

I went cold inside, but I still kept Andrew's secret.

We went down to Brighton to visit Andrew the summer at the end of his first year. He'd decided to stay on after the end of term to earn some extra money. Ken said he could have found Andrew something to do. Andrew insisted that he would rather stay in Brighton, as his accommodation had to be paid for all year round anyway. Getting value for money – that was something Ken understood.

Brighton wasn't far from the seaside town where we still took our holidays, every year in the last two weeks of July, and so I suggested that we went to visit on our way home. Ken contacted the AA to get a route plan from their Home Routes Service, and studied it for days before we left, cross-referencing it with his Readers Digest/AA New Book of the Road.

We met Andrew at a café not far from the sea. There was a black and white photo on the wall of young men and women – they looked like they were students – holding placards saying things like 'Glad to be gay' and 'Homosexuals claim the right to love'. A handwritten piece of card pinned below, curling at the edges, said 'Sussex Gay Liberation Front's Gay Day, 28th October 1972'. Next to it was a mimeographed September 1985 programme for The Beverly Hills private members club and a card with the number for the Brighton Gay Switchboard.

I guided Ken into a seat so that he had his back to all this – that was a conversation I really wanted to avoid. Then I had to steer him away from how many young men there were in the café, how long their hair was, and how that with all the young women with short hair he couldn't tell which ones were the girls and which ones were the boys.

I was in the middle of all of this when a slight young man with a lovely smile and a name tag saying 'Brian' came to take our order. I didn't recognise some of the things on the menu. I knew Ken was just about to comment, so I talked over him to ask for a pot of tea for two and two toasted teacakes. As Brian walked away, Ken pointed out Brian's CND badge and started to mutter about young people today. I saw Andrew walking up to the café and waved, really hoping that Ken would change the subject.

It was an exhausting lunch. Ken kept on finding things to notice. I kept on trying to redirect him. Andrew was quiet and strained, and the slight young man kept a concerned eye on him. At the end, Andrew said that he wanted to tell us something. He said that he needed us to know that he was gay, and that he was sharing a bedsit with a man, here in Brighton. I looked across at the slight young man, who flushed, and smiled as reassuringly as I could. I thought he looked nice.

Andrew's secret was no longer mine to keep.

Ken went pale, and then flushed red. I thought he was about to shout, but instead he grabbed my arm and told me that we were going. *If You Love Somebody Set Them Free* played as the door shut behind us.

He was silent as we walked to the car, and then pretty much all the way home. He only started talking when we pulled into the drive.

His voice was quiet and tense. He asked if I knew and had been keeping it from him. He said that we weren't to tell anyone. That it was just a phase. That Andrew would grow out of it. And that the neighbours and his family must never know.

He never spoke about it again.

Andrew sat between us as a secret.

Of course, I kept in touch with Andrew. He was my son. I visited when I could, telling Ken that I was going to see my sister who lived in London. I think he believed me. Perhaps he just pretended he did. I don't think I'll ever know.

I got to know Brian, the young man in the café, and found out that my first impression had been right. That he was nice. Actually, I discovered that he was everything I wanted in a partner for Andrew., though I had to admit to myself I would have liked grandchildren. And I wished they could have had an easier life, especially as the news of the gay disease emerged from America.

Andrew's letter arrived the day after I got that awful call from the police. Just two and a half years after he left to go to Brighton and a few months before he would have finished his teaching degree. I kept a copy of it in my pocket – I didn't want the original to get spoiled, so the lady in the library made two photocopies for me.

The letter was short. That he was sorry. That Brian had developed AIDS and his death had been slow. Horrible. Brutal. That he had tested HIV-positive, and he couldn't live any longer wondering if every ache or pain, every rash and stomach upset was the beginning of it all for him. That he just couldn't do it alone.

I'm doing all right. It hurts – it will always hurt – but I'm managing. What I can't manage is Ken. He won't talk. Won't admit that he is grieving. Last week, he finally allowed me to put up a picture of Andrew in the hall, but he won't let me put one up in the living room.

I'm already dreading Christmas and it's only June.

10

Agnes: I will not be a closet mother

I will not be a closet mother.

My son was gay. He died. It broke my heart.

But I will not pretend he died of cancer or pneumonia.

He died of AIDS.

I will sew the quilt for him.

I will march at Pride with his boyfriend.

I will hold the hands of the boys whose parents do not visit the hospital.

I will protect them from family members who call to tell them that it's God's punishment.

I will be the shoulder to cry on for the nurses who keep the midnight vigils.

I will let no-one die alone.

I will comfort their friends.

I will not be a closet mother.

11

Nancy: A place of safety

My mum called it a place of safety. I didn't understand that then. As far as I was concerned it was just a holiday. A chance to escape from the city and hang out with a bunch of kids in a big house in the country. I loved it.

Growing up in the 1980s, there was a lot of rubbish going around about HIV and AIDS. The girls at my Catholic school whispered about who had it and how they got it. There were so many stories – I guess they would be called urban legends or conspiracy theories now. That you could get it from toilet seats, doorknobs, swimming pools, kissing, insect bites. Using the same knife and fork as someone who had it. That it had come about because God didn't like gay people. And what made it worse, I see now, is that the grown-ups didn't want to talk to the kids about it. They thought not knowing would keep us innocent and safe. They didn't hear what I heard in the toilets at school.

Thankfully, my mum was different.

I'd lived all my life in the very adult environment of a pub, and I guess it gave me a different perspective on the world. And then on top of that, you add having a mum training to be an AIDS counsellor. There were copies of the *Pink Pages* and safe sex leaflets on the kitchen table, rather than the latest issue of *Woman's Own*. Instead of a calendar with kittens on the wall, there was a poster about how, even when you have only slept with one person, you are basically having sex with everyone they have slept with. Not as cute, I know. But perhaps more useful.

Sex education at my school was patchy to say the least, but unless you had a mum like mine, it was all we had. The nuns had cut all the pages on contraception out of the books, and instead they told us about all the gross historical stuff, like backstreet abortions and women dying in childbirth. It wasn't really surprising that they didn't mention anything about AIDS or any other sexually transmitted diseases. I think they thought they could scare us into abstinence.

When I told my mum about our so-called sex ed lessons, she was furious. She always said that unplanned pregnancies weren't ideal, but there are ways to deal with them. But that AIDS was a death sentence – it really was, at the time – and there was no way to deal with that. According to her, the best way to prevent things was to understand them, and that needed to be before, not after, because once you are in a situation where sex might happen, it's too late to learn about it then. And of course, sex isn't always consensual.

I became Mum's information source for her training. She would ask me to tell her what the girls talked about at school. At first it was really awkward – I mean, who wants to talk to their mum about sex? – but after a while, it was just what we did. And we laughed a lot. I told her that they thought you couldn't get pregnant if you jumped up and down after sex, if you had sex standing up, or it was the first time you'd done it. That only gay men or people who slept around got sexually transmitted diseases. That you couldn't get an STD from oral sex. That if you douched or washed after sex, you couldn't get an STD, and if he pulled out, you wouldn't get pregnant. There were at least two girls in my year who proved that last one wrong. One sat her exams eight and a half months pregnant, and another redid the year with a baby at home.

Mum never judged anyone on their sexuality or their sex life. She just wanted people to know the risks and protect themselves. For her, Catholicism was about what you did, not what you said. Something you lived, in order to benefit society. This included volunteering at the summer camp for people and families affected by HIV and AIDS. It also saw her going to gay clubs and drag shows to fundraise and spread information, and to hand out condoms, leaflets and badges.

The clubs and bars were brilliant. They loved her. They held auctions for everything from a David Hockney painting to a Star Trek kilt. I dressed up in a giant teddy costume and went round with a bucket. I was given chocolate and feather boas by a drag artist, who taught me how to do perfect eyeliner and gave me my favourite lipstick. And I learned that tucking wasn't just something you did with a bed sheet.

And then there was the summer camp, and I looked forward to it every year. It was open to everyone. Parents and carers with babies born HIV-positive, who were growing into toddlers with AIDS. Men infected by a blood transfusion, whose neighbours kept saying they 'must have been up to something'. Kids who were healthy, but one of their two dads had AIDS. Teenagers who had a mum who was HIV-positive because their dad had had an affair, or a big sister who tested positive after a needlestick injury at the hospital where she nursed. Children whose dad had told the neighbours that their big brother, who developed AIDS after he had shared a needle, had died from lymphoma.

To others they were people who had 'brought it on themselves' – or hadn't. People who were 'guilty' or 'innocent'. To me, they were just families on holiday, with kids I played with every summer.

Coming to camp was their place of safety, where no-one would ask, and no-one would tell. That meant I never knew who was sick and who wasn't. It also meant that the kids got to just be kids. HIV wasn't the centre of it. Messing around and having fun was. And making friends for life. However long that life might be. Because it was where I learned that not just old people die, it could be people my age and so much younger.

Mum found me crying my heart out one year on the bridge over the stream. I told her it was where I'd taught one of the little ones Poohsticks the year before and he hadn't come back. She held me and rocked me like I was a baby, and we played Poohsticks for Peter and his mum.

When some of the young gay men coming to camp for the first time met my mum – a straight white Catholic who was the same age as their parents – they would set out to shock her. I remember hearing her asking someone what they wanted to do first. He said, 'I want to go cottaging', expecting her to get all embarrassed. Instead, quick as a flash, she said 'Hop in the car then, I know the best places.' I guess they were doing it to check out her motivation or see if she would judge. But as one of the longest serving landladies in Yorkshire, my mum knew not to judge, how not to be shocked (or at least how not to *look* shocked), and how to give as good as she got.

The summer camp was held in a big old house with everything from rooms where you could chill out to people who would give you a massage. There were always doctors on hand, as some people were really ill, and counsellors who could provide specialist in-depth support. And there was always something to do. A game of cards. Board games. Playing football. Hide & seek. Arts and crafts. Computer games – well, *3D Monster Maze* and *Fungaloids* on a ZX81 hooked up to a black and white portable TV and a tape recorder. Fun stuff. We even had a fashion show one year where we tried on each other's clothes and made the grownups watch as we strutted around in borrowed high heels,. Seeing who could walk the furthest before they fell over in hysterics. My mum and the other volunteers tried to make things as ordinary as they could for the families and their kids, and it really was, even down to arguments about who's been on the computer the longest – this was the late eighties, after all, and loading up a game from a cassette was slooooow.

The adults talked to my mum about symptoms, the impact on their families, how afraid they were. About the graffiti on their houses. The letters, and worse, pushed through their letterboxes. And the supposedly 'moral' people writing to headteachers and signing petitions to demand that certain kids were taken out of school.

I looked after the kids. Did the head counts on trips out to Flamingoland and Alton Towers, and went down log flumes. Went scrambling across the countryside and got chased by a bull. I ended up lifting armfuls of kids over the wall, and then scrambled over and fell in the nettles, only to see my best friend calmly walking through the gate. And I was supposed to be the responsible one...

The kids talked to me. Told me things that they didn't always tell their parents. Notes in their school bags, bullies calling them awful names, houses they weren't allowed to visit, teachers who wouldn't come near them. And I knew enough to answer some of their questions about symptoms, or how to (or not to) spread the virus. Like my mum, I learned how not to be shocked.

When some people learned that mum took me to the camp and asked why she would allow me to share cups with 'those people', she was furious. And what she said wasn't printable, because of course she wouldn't ever have put me in a situation that she didn't think was safe. And it wasn't the people you might expect to be uptight – the ones at church – they were brilliant. It was the people who thought they were worldly and open minded. Mum and Dad's friends. Customers from the pub.

I knew to be careful with blood. Anyone's blood. There were blanket rules for everyone, so no-one was put on the spot. All cuts had to be covered, and no-one was allowed to work in the kitchen without gloves, or if they had a sore or a graze on their hands, arms or faces.

My mum was – and still is – such an advocate. I love that she was brave enough to stand up and stand out. A straight woman dealing with what people called the Gay Disease – something that didn't necessarily need to involve her. But she always saw it as so much more than just a gay issue. She wasn't the one being victimised. But like all human rights, when you see yourself as human first, it involves all of us.

I learned so much from her, and from the camps. It's the reason that I am who I am and that I do what I do, supporting families with disabled children and training to be a Children and Young People's Wellbeing therapist.

In some ways I have come full circle. I like to think I provide a place of safety.

12

Emma: Long shadows

I was born angry.

No, that's not true. I wasn't.

I was born loved. I *became* angry.

I lost my entire family when I was very young. My dad died when I was a year old, and my mum and my baby sister over the next 18 months. I have scraps of memories, but I'm not sure whether they are real. They have the odd pink tinge of old photographs.

People tell me that I'm lucky. That I'm healthy. That I had family that took me in and loved me. Even that I should be grateful that I lost them so young.

When I was a small child, all I knew was that I didn't have a mummy and daddy and that Jen and Tom were like my mummy and daddy. This didn't make me angry, just curious. I wondered who I might be. Perhaps I was a princess who had to be kept safe from an evil wizard. Later I thought I might be the daughter of a famous actor who hadn't been able to acknowledge me but would come and whisk me away one day. I scrutinised the faces in Jen's magazines to see who might look like me.

When Jen heard me telling the babysitter that my parents were spies – I have no idea how I even knew what a spy was – and they had to keep me secret, she and Tom sat me down and explained that my mum was her cousin and that my mum and my dad and baby sister had died. Like our cat Tibby. I took this very calmly, apparently. Later, Jen found me in the garden digging with my tiny sandcastle spade, and I told her I was looking to see if they were down there with the cat.

I wasn't angry then. It was just a thing, and I knew that Tom and Jen loved me, and I loved them.

I learned the truth at school. Or a version of it.

I was thirteen. In what used to be called the third year, the year where you choose your subjects for O-levels.

Sarah James was the popular girl. Every school has one. The one with the right haircut, the right shoes, the right bag. Even her school uniform was somehow more 'right' than anyone else's. I sat next to her in class. She seemed to like me. And I basked in her reflected glory.

One morning, in registration in our form room, she moved her chair to the other end of the desk, sticking right out into the aisle. Everyone turned round to look. Miss Jenkins told her to move back, and she said that she wouldn't, because she might catch something. Miss Jenkins told her not to be silly, and to move her chair back immediately. She did, but she sat as far across on the seat as she could, with her back half turned away from me. At break time and at lunchtime, no-one spoke to me, but there was a lot of staring, whispering and pointing.

I wasn't angry then. I just thought I must have done something wrong.

I tried to talk to her, and she shouted at me to go away. Said that my dad was a gay and a dirty druggie and he and my mum had died of AIDS, and they had killed my sister. That if they'd died of AIDS, I must have it. And if anyone touched me, they would get AIDS too – in fact, I'd probably already given it to everyone in all our classes, and they were all going to die.

I wasn't angry then. I was just scared that I might be capable of killing someone.

Miss Jenkins found me sobbing in the school nurse's room. I told her what had happened. She called Jen, and I sat in the library until I could go home. Tucked up on the sofa together with cocoa and marshmallows, Jen said she was sorry that she hadn't told me before, but she had wanted to wait until I was a bit older.

She explained that my dad had been a lovely man, and that he liked men more than he liked women. He hadn't been allowed to marry the man he loved. He liked my mum very much – she was his best friend – and so they got married. He'd been happy at first, but he got more and more unhappy, and instead of talking to the doctor he had taken drugs to make himself feel better. He took more and more drugs, and when they stopped working, he injected heroin. And he must have used a dirty needle, because he got infected with HIV. He'd kept everything secret from my mum, though now I wonder if she was in denial, because I'm not sure that you can actually hide something like that.

Dad didn't get tested for HIV until he started to get ill. It was only then that she found out that she and the new baby both had the virus too. My dad and my little sister died of pneumonia and my mum died of cancer.

I blurted out what Sarah had said about me having it and passing it on to everyone at school. And what if she and Tom got it from me and they died too? She hugged me tight and told me not to be daft. That I had been tested when my mum and sister were ill, and my tests were negative. I cried and her cheek was wet.

I wasn't angry then, because Jen was angry for me. And that made me feel warm inside. Or it might have been the cocoa. But I don't think the fear ever quite went away.

Miss Jenkins must have talked to the class, because when I went back in the next day, there was no name calling. Sarah still managed to make my life a misery. Never quite enough to get her into trouble, but enough to make me quiet and sad.

I sat alone for the rest of the school year. I never got a partner for any projects, or if I did, they kept as far away from me as they could.

And I started to get angry.

I moved to a new secondary school on the other side of town, away from Sarah and her friends, where the head teacher had been told what had happened. The teachers were kind, and it was a fresh start, but I withdrew. Didn't talk much. Didn't try to make friends. If people asked about my parents, I just talked about the how. The cancer and the pneumonia. Not the why.

For a while, people left me alone. For almost the whole of the school year. But the stories about my dad had somehow followed me, and they spread around the school like wildfire when I went back after Easter. I became even more angry. Angry that he had been stupid enough to catch the virus, angry that I had to keep it a secret and angry that people found out anyway, however hard I tried.

After the last year of being the one on the receiving end, I took back the power. I started by taking it out on the bullies. And then I became the bully.

I made people too afraid of me to speak up. I could hurt without leaving marks. It wasn't just about my strength, though. My voice could cause as much pain as my hands.

I got away with it. So, I carried on. And the teachers didn't seem to notice – I kept quiet in class, and being neither particularly clever nor particularly stupid and not letting my work slip meant I didn't attract any attention.

I also managed to hide it from Jen and Tom. Until one day I couldn't, when a furious father arrived on the doorstep, telling them what I had done.

I was angry that he had come into my home and made accusations. That the accusations were true didn't seem to matter to me. All that mattered in that moment was me and how unfair everything was.

They tried to talk to me, and I ran to my room. Locked the door. I could hear them downstairs. Not the actual words, just a hurt and confused rumble of voices, interspersed by Jen's tears and the man's raised voice. I put a record on loud to drown it all out, and then, when it finished, I lay there listening to the click of the needle at the end of the groove, and then the silence. Eventually, I must have fallen asleep, fully dressed.

I woke up to a ringing phone the next morning, late, groggy and confused. Jen and Tom came to my room.

There had been complaints. A lot of them. The school was suspending me for the final two weeks of term and would decide whether I would be allowed back in September. I tried to laugh it off, saying that at least it meant I didn't need to sit my mocks, but Jen and Tom kept silent. They weren't angry. They were sad. Disappointed. And that somehow made it all worse.

I wanted them to shout. To hurt me. To make me feel like the girls I had bullied, so I could be righteously angry.

I couldn't keep all the pain and hurt in, and instead of asking for help, I lashed out. Told them I wished they'd never taken me in. That I hated them. That it was a good thing they'd never been able to have children, because their children would be as messed up as me. That I wished I'd died like my sister. That I wished I'd never been born. Then I ran back to my room and listened to loud music and cried until I fell asleep.

This cycle continued for days. I was grounded. Not that it really mattered. There wasn't anywhere I wanted to go or anyone I wanted to see, or who wanted to see me. I'd wait until Jen and Tom left for work before I got up. We would eat together in silence when they got home. I would pick a fight. I'd go up to my room and cry. Lather, rinse, repeat. But with added fury and not as many bubbles.

A couple of weeks after the visit from the girl's father, Tom walked into my room. He put a suitcase on my bed and told me to pack for a week, as we were going away, and if I wouldn't pack, he would pack for me. His face suggested that he would brook no arguments, and I was too exhausted anyway.

We drove for an hour and ended up at a big old house in the country, with a whole lot of strangers. At first I stayed in my room. Sulked like a toddler. Saw Jen and Tom smile in a way that I hadn't seen for weeks. They dropped food off for me but didn't hang around. Left me to my own devices. Eventually, boredom and curiosity took me downstairs.

A girl my age saw me hesitating at the bottom of the stairs and smiled. She told me that her name was Nancy, and she knew that

I must be Emma. I looked hard at her, expecting her to say what she'd heard about me, but she just beckoned me through into a messy, sunny room. There were bigger kids playing board games, little kids doing jigsaws, and a teenage boy and girl arguing over a computer game. I sat in an old, overstuffed armchair in the furthest corner and grabbed the nearest book I could see to hide behind. It was Susan Cooper's *Over Sea, Under Stone* and I got lost in the Grey House.

I was so far away in deepest Cornwall that it was only when I felt a tap on my shoulder that I noticed that all of the others had gone. A woman with a kind face sat on the chair next to me. She explained about the summer camp – that it was for families like mine who had been affected by HIV, including those who had lost people and those who were infected. She told me that everyone else had gone into tea, but she wondered if I would like to talk to her for a bit.

Over the next few days, she and I talked a lot. It didn't take the pain and hurt away. I don't think anything ever will. But I think I started to learn how to ask for help. Tom and Jen came to a couple of the sessions too. But the camp wasn't all talking, which was a relief. I'm not good at that. Sometimes I'm better at silence. It was about getting swept into what Jen called the feral pack. We ran in the fields and climbed trees. We even got chased by a bull. I had the best time because nobody looked at me or treated me any differently.

Jen and Tom went home, but the people running the camp asked me if I would like to stay on to help out for the second week. I made some amazing friends that summer.

Going home was hard because I knew I would have to face Jen and Tom again, and we would have to work out what was going to happen with school in September.

Looking back now, I have had to learn to deal with who I am, because that was never going to be fixed by a couple of counselling sessions and a summer away.

I used to say that I was born angry, but I wasn't. I was born loved.

I became angry when life dealt me this hand. And anger has a long shadow.

A long, silent shadow.

13

Angela: A week away at the seaside

I think it was a Sunday afternoon when Jenny rang from London. I had to tell her to slow down and catch her breath. She said it was Alex, and my immediate thought was, 'what's wrong?'

I'd never met Alex, but she'd talked about him so much I felt like I had. I'd seen pictures of Jenny and her girlfriend out with John and Alex in London, all very glamorous, and they sent me postcards from their wonderful holidays abroad. As a mum with a newborn, I can't pretend I wasn't ever jealous, but it was nice to see beautiful people having a lovely time in sun-soaked places. I stuck the Polaroids and postcards up on the fridge with 'Present from The Lakes' magnets.

Jenny finally slowed down and caught her breath. Alex had got a diagnosis. And not just a diagnosis, *the* diagnosis. And it was hardly surprising that he was devastated. He'd always been 'a bit of a one' according to Jenny, but he and John had been together for a year or so. Perhaps they thought they were safe.

Jenny had asked him what he needed, and he said he needed to get away. She'd promised them somewhere to stay by the sea, but her mum, who lived a few streets away from me, had freaked out and Jenny was really shocked. She'd thought her parents were more open-minded than that, and they ended up having a huge row. So... would we have Alex and John to stay for a week?

After a whispered conversation with my husband Ed, which I suspect Jenny heard every word of, we said yes. I mean, what else could we say?

About an hour later, after congratulating ourselves for being marvellous, we had a small panic. I mean – was it safe, with a baby in the house? Ed had the bright idea of talking to someone at the Terrence Higgins Trust. Directory Enquiries has always been business-like, but there was definitely a little pause when he asked for the Trust's number.

The lovely woman on the end of the phone at the Trust let Ed talk at ninety miles an hour, and then, very calmly, gave us good advice. This was long before being able to put phones on speaker, and I had my ear squished right up against his. What she said boiled down to 'just treat them as normal people' and 'be careful if there is any blood'. We grinned at each other. We could manage that.

We had a tiny terraced house with a view of the sea from the top bedroom if you stood on one leg and leaned sideways a bit. There was only just space for me, my husband and the baby, so we begged and borrowed an airbed and bedding.

When they arrived fresh off the train from London, these two beautiful boys from the city with suitcases and shirts and ties and totally impractical shoes, they were on their best behaviour. Please and thank you and as straight as you like. But by the end of the week, they were as camp as a row of flowery tents.

They were so shocked at the lack of food – we were young and skint and working silly hours as well as dealing with a baby – that they filled the fridge with healthy foods. They also covered every inch of work surface in the tiny galley kitchen with pills and potions and vitamins and flowers, and added Polaroids of the four of us and the baby to the fridge. When they went home, visibly more relaxed and with a bit of Yorkshire colour in their cheeks, they left a thank-you note in Alex's lovely handwriting – I recognised it straight away from the postcards – inviting us to their flat in 'the metrolops'. He added his phone number and told us that we were now allowed to let the fridge empty and hide the ashtrays.

Listening to them talk about what they'd seen and done while they were here made me look at what I had with fresh eyes. I might not have had nightclubs and amazing restaurants and exotic holidays, but I did have the glory of the North Yorkshire coast. I could see the sea from my bedroom (sort of), and I could walk on the beach every day. Though there were still days I looked at the postcards and thought longingly about a tequila sunrise and a bit of heat.

14

Jenny: Icebergs and exploding mountains

When I think of those years, I think of the adverts with icebergs and tombstones and exploding mountains and John Hurt. The press and the government creating an environment of blame and fear. And people getting so scared.

In the early days of the crisis, we got a lot of calls at the AIDS helpline from the worried well, usually straight. People who thought they might have caught it from touching a toothbrush or by using a glass that hadn't been washed properly. From a hug, a kiss, a handshake, an insect bite. Sharing communion wine. One day I even had a caller who was terrified his son might have caught it from a toilet fixed by an allegedly gay plumber.

I could go on. Pour me another glass of wine and I probably will.

Yes, I know they were ordinary people who didn't understand and were frightened. I know they needed compassion. And I was usually very good at being kind. But some days I just had to hide in the toilet and scream into a towel.

As the crisis went on, and I guess as people understood more, those worried well largely faded away, which was a relief. Less screaming into towels. Instead, calls from the people who really needed our help. Those left me sobbing into said towel instead. I got through a lot of towels in those years.

People asked about symptoms, wanted to know where they could get support. Reliable tests finally came out, but as treatment still wasn't widely available, they wanted to ask our advice on whether it was worth getting tested. It was a hard choice to make. Some just wanted to know, others were worried that if it got out that they were positive they could be kicked out of their home or sacked from their job.

Some days it felt like the Samaritans. The young HIV-positive man who thought that he'd infected his late partner and was eaten up with guilt. The lonely men whose partners had died but there was no support for them. The man who told me that he was HIV-negative and felt like he didn't fit in with his community any longer.

I got to a point that I couldn't take any more, even with all the towels in the world. I escaped London, leaving everything behind – my friends, the helpline, my job, my flatmate – to find sea and sun and work where I could top up both my tan and my Spanish. Looking back now, it seems really selfish, but at the time I just needed to get away.

I knew that my lovely friend Alex was HIV-positive, but I don't think I took on board how quickly his illness could progress. Perhaps I was in denial. So, the news coming down a crackling phone line in the hotel lobby was a huge shock. Alex was in hospital. My world spun. I threw all my clothes into a bag, tossed my keys at the reception desk and ran for the taxi rank.

I got to the hospital in time. Such a relief. Alex was asleep, tended by a nurse who was sheathed in plastic from head to toe. For an awful moment I wanted to laugh at what seemed to be a human in a condom.

Alex had been such a beautiful man and here he was, just a shadow. Looking like a skeleton carved out of marble. He woke up when I sat down and we talked through the night in between his sudden and uneasy naps, times where I wasn't sure whether he was asleep or unconscious. He was furious about what had happened to him and truly did rage against the dying of his light. He didn't want to die, and I hated people telling me it would be a blessed release. It wouldn't be. He would have given anything still to be here.

The next call was about Alison, the first woman I knew to die of AIDS. She was bisexual and had come out in her forties after her abusive marriage broke up. She was just enjoying herself after so many years of unhappiness. Her latest partner didn't want to use a condom, and she thought everything would be fine. She was on the pill, after all. I don't know whether he had any idea that he was HIV-positive. I really hope he didn't, because that would make me more furious than I can manage. She had night sweats, aches, memory loss, thrush and issues with concentration and jokingly brushed these off as the menopause.

And then there was Adrian. We had worked on the helpline together, and he had no illusions of what he would go through, so he chose dying by suicide rather than what he called the AIDS death by a thousand cuts. I went to his inquest, where the coroner asked his partner whether they had 'been intimate' that day and whether they had any 'normal' friends.

I never knew when the next call would come. When the next taxi would be at the door. When the next funeral would be. It felt like blow after blow after blow, and as if no-one outside of our community actually cared.

15

Sylvia: Acting up for attention

I did so much that summer in the late 80s, the year I escaped London to get away from all the death. My friend Jenny and I decided to hitch down through Europe in search of sun. We got to Barcelona. I stopped there and she carried on further south, aiming for Malaga or Marbella – something beginning with an M on the coast, anyway.

I'd been in Barcelona for a few days, looking for work in the bars and somewhere cheap to stay, when I met a totally drop-dead gorgeous English woman called Carol. She made my toes tingle. That night Carol took me back to her flat, and – well – I didn't really leave.

Carol swept me into her world. She took me to her lesbian choir, which sang feminist songs at conferences and scared straight women, and pulled me into the Barcelona chapter of ACT UP - the AIDS Coalition to Unleash Power.

ACT UP was political and beautiful and radical and completely glorious. Our goal was to act up and act out to create publicity about the AIDS pandemic. We were non-violent but more than happy to be as civilly disobedient as possible to get people to look at us, to see what was going on under their noses.

The first thing Carol and I did together was plaster the city in the ACT UP Barcelona posters of coffins. We tiptoed around the warm dark streets with buckets of paste and long-handled brushes, sticking up the posters and trying not to giggle too loudly. When we were done, we ran back to our flat to shower off the stickiness and the heat and drink beer into the small hours.

One Saturday she and I joined a group of twenty or thirty people dressed in white. We put on blank, pale Venetian masks and stalked down the middle of Las Ramblas, shouting, 'Silence kills!' Tourists took photographs, drivers shook their fists at us, young men laughed, and old men watched curiously from bars, cigarettes in hand.

The biggest event of the year was the protest outside the hospital. People with AIDS were dying without proper treatment or support, and no-one seemed to know or care. So, we decided that we would make them take notice, by setting up a 'die-in'.

We marched on the hospital, Mothers, friends, lovers and allies. Protesting the rights of people with AIDS in hospital, from proper food to emotional support. When we got there, we laid down across the pavement holding our placards under a huge banner that asked: 'How many people with AIDS will you let die handcuffed in this hospital?' Other protesters drew chalk outlines around us – when we got up it looked like the aftermath of a crime scene.

At the end of the summer Carol went back to England, and I stayed on in the flat. It wasn't a big fight or anything, it was just how things worked out.

Just last year, a friend sent me a pamphlet that he found in his drawer. It described ACT UP as 'lying in the road, telephone-blocking, fax-zapping, letter-writing, informing, condom-dropping, researching, lobbying, talking, shouting, screaming, stickering, misbehaving, lying-in, dying-in, painting, retaliating, creating and having fun.'

That was pretty much what we were about, and it really was fun. I so hope we made a difference.

16

Charlotte: The Chicken Soup Brigade

I've got a friend in Seattle. Angela. Well, she's a friend of a friend of a friend, and I can't quite remember how we started as penfriends, but we've been writing for years.

I've got a drawer full of those wispy blue airmail letters that you fold together like origami, where we've shared everything from what we have for breakfast to our coming-out stories.

When she first moved to the West Coast in 1979, she wanted to get involved in the local community, and she started volunteering at the Seattle Gay Clinic that had just opened up in the city. A few years later – 1983, I think – she told me about a buddy group she'd got involved with. It had a brilliant name – The Chicken Soup Brigade – because everyone knows how good chicken soup is when you don't feel well. They helped out people who were ill, doing shopping – 'going to the store', she said – or getting them to a doctor's appointment. They would walk dogs, clean toilets, write letters, even raise money to get people home for Christmas. Anything that was needed, really.

In another letter, she said that the group had got involved in working with people with AIDS. At the time, we hadn't seen much of it here, other than frightening and over-the-top headlines and awful rumours, but she saw it unfolding day by day at the clinic. I learned so much from her letters. The real brutal truth. The days that seemed to be filled with men wasting away, with their hands trembling and their skins covered with bluish-purple lesions. Men who were skeletal but proud, with kitchen tables covered in drugs but no food in the fridge. Men who had given up. One day she let herself into a flat – I can't get used to calling them apartments – and saw the man she was there to visit sobbing on his sofa, a mirror and a photograph next to him. 'I used to be so beautiful,' he said, 'and now look at me.'

It wasn't awful all the time, though. She was told all the glorious stories and scurrilous gossip of the gay scene in Seattle. Heard about politicians so far in the closet they were in Narnia, and learned all about art, music and theatre. She told me about the men she visited, sad and furious and stoic, who were so pleased to see her and thanked her all the time through their tears and fury. Best of all, which left me giggling for days, was the story about the day she moved a piece of furniture to sweep underneath and watched an entire hidden box of 'toys' tumble down the stairs. Or the time she was asked to read old love letters and they got really graphic.

At the Chicken Soup Brigade office, Angela met a woman called Carol Sterling, a self-described 'loudmouth lesbian,' who got her excited about civil rights. Carol and the Chicken Soup Brigade helped to stop evictions and found people new accommodation.

The thing that made Angela most angry, though, were the funeral homes who refused to take the bodies of people who died of AIDS, or who were overcharging desperate and heartbroken families. Angela would go down to the funeral homes like an avenging angel. Funeral directors took to disappearing through the back door when she went in the front, leaving their minions to take the full force of a red-headed New Yorker in army boots.

Angela and I finally met face-to-face in the noughties when I saved up enough to travel to America, and we are still in touch now, though it's emails and video calls now rather than letters. She was my rock when my wife died, and I'm the long-distance Goddess-mother for her daughter and grandson. We talk every few weeks, but I have to admit I do rather miss the click of the letterbox and the waft of those thin blue letters onto the doormat.

17

Anne: It's okay, take your time

Ever since I heard Sarah Mulligan shout 'lezzer' across the playground, all I wanted to do was get away. Go to **the** London. The one I read about in those books hidden under my bed. Those so few books that talked about how women could love women, and it was all okay. So, I went to the tech and got my Pitman shorthand and typing, saved every penny from my Saturday job at Woolworths, packed my case, found a bedsit, signed up with a temp agency, and waited for my life to begin as the best dyke in London.

And I waited.

And I waited.

Because I had no idea where the dykes were. They weren't in the shared kitchen with a grubby fridge full of food that I didn't recognise. They weren't in the shiny offices full of men who either patronised me or tried to look down my top. And they certainly weren't in the local pub that stank of smoke and beer and old men and old men's old dogs.

I called my mum from the phone box. Told her everything was wonderful, that I was eating properly, had lots of friends. And that's when I saw it.

The ad.

London Gay Switchboard. 24-hour information & advice.

A gentle voice.

'Hello. What would you like to talk about this evening? It's okay, take your time.'

I thought I wanted to ask where the nearest women-only bar was, but I realised that I actually just wanted to talk. To ask whether I was dyke enough to go to a gay bar and talk to real grown-up dykes. Whether they would just laugh at me and throw me out because I didn't look enough like a dyke in my Littlewoods suit and Dolcis heels and Tammy Girl flares. Because I didn't own any comfortable shoes or dungarees. Because they would be able to see, instantly, that I'd kissed a boy and never kissed a girl. Because I wouldn't pass the dyke test.

I put the phone down.

Two weeks later I rang up again.

'Hello.'

Another gentle voice. A woman this time.

And the floodgates opened. I filled the phone with ten pence pieces, and her ears with my teenage heartbreak. When I finally stopped, there was a silence. I thought she was going to laugh. But she didn't.

'Oh, love. Don't you worry. There's no test. There's just people.'

I found the Drill Hall. The Fallen Angel. Venus Rising at the Fridge. The Duke of Wellington. 48 Club at Reeves Hotel. Gingers at Spats. The Ace of Clubs on Piccadilly. Below Stairs and the women-only floor at the London Lesbian and Gay Centre. The bar at First Out Café.

I found my people, my tribe, my comfortable shoes. I found a girl I wanted to kiss, and who wanted to kiss me.

And then one day I called Switchboard again.

'Hello. I want to volunteer.'

I had no idea what that would actually mean, though.

In that tiny office above a bookshop in King's Cross, smelling of smoke and last night's poppers and Beanfeast Mexican Chilli, we had all the calls. The drunken hoax calls. The guy in the bar who fancied a man on the dance floor but who couldn't remember the handkerchief-in-the-back-pocket code. The homophobes telling us that we were all going to hell. The women who – like me – had moved to London and wanted to know where to hang out. We recorded them all in A4 notebooks, along with questions to each other, pleas for gay-friendly accommodation, arguments about who stole whose sandwiches from the fridge, and notes about where the police were raiding that night. The notebooks got more and more battered and filled with flyers as the months went by, until someone gave in and bought a new one.

I learned about things I never knew existed, and got very good at never sounding surprised. And I learned about HIV/AIDS. Gay-Related Immune Deficiency, as it was sometimes still called. Or worse – horrible, offensive, homophobic playground slurs.

The callers were silent. Or weeping. Or angry. Or all of them. And they were all scared. And increasingly, they were dying. My gorgeous, glorious best friend Christopher, who sat opposite me on the phones, started to get thinner. Lose the glow to his perfect skin. He told me he didn't need to be tested. That he had the flu. That he'd been trying to lose a few pounds. That he was having a go at being vegan. But I knew. And he knew that I knew.

Over the next few months, the phones at Switchboard were taken over by women as the men got sick, or as they left to care for their partners. The call numbers rose with every news report, every documentary, every airing of that awful 'Don't Die of Ignorance' ad campaign with its tombstone and lilies. In between temping to pay the rent I spent every hour on the phones or sitting with Christopher. Caring for him. I was only 25, and I was watching my 23-year-old best friend die.

Over those next few years, I was at a funeral every week. Full of colour and drag queens and stories and tears mixed with laughter. The weeping, confused family members who'd had to deal with the coming out of their child on the day of his death. The strains of The Communards' *For a Friend* as the too-light coffin left.

I loved and lost and loved again.

We still get the calls from people who are afraid of the virus, but it's thankfully nothing like it was.

'Hello. What would you like to talk about this evening? It's okay, take your time.'

18

Cathy: Listening in the silences

The helpline room was an odd mixture of silence and noise. The street outside was constantly busy, starting with the late-night people leaving the pubs to go to the clubs, and ending with the early morning cleaners calling to each other and laughing as they slammed the office doors. In between were the sirens, and the prostitutes looking for their last punter before they went to sleep the day away. Inside, if I was there alone and the phone wasn't ringing, there was a heavy, dull, anticipatory quiet, broken by the gurgles of the heating, the click of the cooling kettle and the hum of the fridge.

When the phone rang and broke the stillness, I never had any idea which kind of call it would be. It's hard to explain how I felt then. A mixture of expectation, anxiety, concern and – I guess – excitement. It may sound odd, but I wouldn't have done it if I hadn't wanted to talk to the callers. On the phones, we went on people's journeys with them, without judgement.

The night callers were a bit of a mixture. Sometimes they were easy, or at the very least, straightforward. Asking for information or providing it. The woman who wanted a recommendation for a lesbian club that was still open, 'as the cow behind the bar had just called last orders far too early.' I knew exactly who she meant, too, and I secretly agreed with her as I looked up the nearest place that would let her in. The daytime helpline volunteer who wanted to know if she'd left her keys behind. She had, and I dropped them off with her flatmate on my way home as she'd found 'alternative accommodation' at The Fallen Angel's women-only night. The gay man, still out of breath after running away, who reported a cottaging site. The man who called again and again until he got a woman on the line and then got himself off – I kept an ACME Thunderer in my drawer for him. The lad who'd had a skinful and was feeling brave enough to make a hoax call. The lad who'd had a skinful and was feeling brave enough to make a call that wasn't a hoax. Sometimes it was the same lad.

But often the night callers were the vulnerable ones. The people who had been stretched so tightly you felt that you would be able to see right through their skin. The teenager kicked out by his stepfather because he'd been caught kissing a boy. The gay man afraid to leave his house because of the verbal abuse he got from his neighbour, but the council wouldn't rehome him and the police wouldn't intervene because they were only words, and he should just ignore them. The man whose mother had told him that she was glad his partner was dead because now he could meet a nice woman and give her grandchildren before he caught that awful gay plague. The woman being abused by her female partner, who was too embarrassed to talk about it because men are abusers, not women.

The silent calls where I just talked quietly and left gaps. Listened in the silences. Told them that it was okay not to talk. That I was there.

And then there were the people who just felt that the world had got too much.

I froze the first time I got a suicide call.

It doesn't matter how much training you've had, you can't prepare yourself for what it will be like.

The caller's voice was quiet. Weak. I had to strain to hear it. He had HIV and he knew he was dying. His boyfriend had died just a few weeks before, and his best friend had gone to his parents, and wasn't likely to come back. He'd taken the pills. He wouldn't tell me where he was. He just wanted company.

We talked for a while. The pauses got longer. And then it went quiet.

Fortunately, I wasn't alone. The other volunteer quietly put down a mug of bitter instant coffee doused with milk on the turn and a touch of cheap whisky. He perched on the corner of the desk. I knew he'd had a similar call a few weeks back. He told me that these were the calls that stay with us. That we can't always know whether we helped or not. He hugged me tight and told me that I should be proud of myself for taking the call and for staying with it. And that at least the last voice that the caller had heard was kind.

It was the first, but it wasn't the last. Sometimes they wouldn't tell me who or where they were. But sometimes they would, and I called 999 and talked until I heard the ambulance men arrive and a kind voice told me that it was okay, they'd got it.

Before I left after a night shift I always peered through the hole in the outside door first, to check that the coast was clear before leaving. We had a fragile relationship with the police, but they had recommended some useful security changes when there were some odd and rather scary people hanging around outside.

Most mornings after I stepped out into the city's faintly grubby early morning sunshine, I headed to the café round the corner. Surrounded by taxi drivers and shift workers, I sank mug after mug of brick-dust-coloured tea from a thick white mug, ate a bacon sandwich made with thick white sliced bread and marge, and let the night's calls slip away.

19

Cat: Near the swimming pool

It had been a long shift, so I was relieved to see Anna come through the door, clutching her rucksack and her pink Tupperware box of neatly-cut cheese sandwiches. She wandered over to the kettle to make an enormous mug of evil-smelling herbal tea. I made a last few notes in the battered A4 call log, reaching over to drop it onto her desk. Both phones rang, and I sat back down with a sigh. Perhaps it would be a quick one, and I wouldn't be too late. She grinned and grabbed the other call.

He said his name was Felix. It might or might not have been. It didn't really matter.

He sounded broken. His partner had died. I sighed inside. Over the last year so many calls started like that. And we were all so very tired.

His partner wasn't out – in fact, he was married with a child. Felix was only ever introduced as a friend, if he was introduced at all. He told me that he couldn't grieve openly. He said that he wasn't even invited to the funeral, and he just stood in the trees in the churchyard like a disenfranchised ghost.

'I'm only 22 but I've seen so many deaths. At my age, most people might have lost a grandparent, but I've lost acquaintances. Friends. Lovers. So many that I don't think I can take it much longer.'

'I'm numb. I'm not even sure that I can be sad or angry anymore. It feels like I've not just lost people, I've lost my way of life, my chance to be young and carefree. I mean – there's no point in being close to anyone else, because they are just going to die on me.'

'I can't go to all the funerals anymore. There are so many. I pick one to go to because of where it is. Near a park, or a friend's house, or the hospital. Or even the shops. And I hate myself for that.'

He rang off. I'd barely said a word. But somehow, he had summed up the whole crisis for me. I hoped that at least talking had helped.

And I set off to my second funeral of the month. It was near the swimming pool.

20

Sharon: An iced bun with a cherry on top

People around me – people at my church who I loved and trusted – told me that I should condemn them. Those people with AIDS. Because the only way that people got the gay plague was through gay sex or drug-taking, and both went against a just and true God. A god who would rightly mete out punishment to the guilty. And that's what I believed.

In the beginning, at least.

Because then there was Matthew. A nine-year-old boy who did none of those things and should have had a whole, amazing life ahead of him.

Matthew was my best friend Sarah's eldest son. Her firstborn and my godson. I'd known him since he was just a bump in Sarah's slender belly. I first held him, all milk-smelling and soft and warm, when he was just a few hours old.

It began with a nosebleed that just wouldn't stop. And then bruising, which got worse when he began to walk. The questions started and the social workers were called in, leaving Sarah terrified that they would threaten to take both him and his newborn baby brother Adrian away. But then Tom, Matthew's cousin, started to get unexplained bruises, and his doctor diagnosed him with haemophilia. Matthew and Adrian were tested, and when they came up positive – well, it was an odd sort of relief for us all.

Matthew went to a residential school with Tom, and Adrian joined them a couple of years later. It was a wonderful place where they made friends who understood. Where they could be monitored and cared for in the on-site haemophilia clinic. And where they were given the new and amazing drug, Factor VIII, harvested from donor blood. It was incredible. A breakthrough. A new and better life where Tom, Matthew and Adrian could run and jump and play and climb, free from aching joints and the risk of bleeding.

I visited Matthew at his school every month or two, and took the three of them out for horrible sticky iced buns with a bright red cherry on top and luridly coloured fizzy drinks – you know, the kinds of things your parents won't let you have, but your godmother will because she is a soft touch. I loved seeing them at school with their friends. One visit, Matthew, in a terrible American accent copied from his beloved Westerns, told me that the Factor VIII came from all over the world, and that his blood would now be American.

We believed the doctors and the government that it was safe. We trusted them.

And then, in 1985 – about a year after they started on the wonder drug – the school doctor school called all the boys with haemophilia into his office. He pointed to them one by one, saying, 'You've got it, you haven't, you two have,' and sent them back to their classes. And Matthew had it. And it was HIV. His younger brother Adrian had hepatitis C. His cousin Tom was free of both viruses. It seemed like some kind of awful raffle.

In 1988, Matthew started to get ill. I visited him in the infectious diseases ward, where the nurses were gloved and gowned and masked, and all the other patients were grown men. I couldn't see him at first, and then I heard him shout my name. He looked so tiny in his hospital bed, with his teddy bear tucked next to him. But even though he was so sick, he still had his charming, cheeky smile. The nurses gave me gloves so that I could hold his hand. I hate that memory now, but then – we still weren't really sure how it was passed on.

I wanted to take him away from there. From the others in the ward. They were the people my church had told me about. The guilty ones.

But they were so kind. The man in the bed one side of him, who came from San Francisco, taught him American slang. The man the other side taught him Polari. I didn't know which country they spoke that, but it made them all laugh. The night nurse read him bedtime stories. The cleaner made a tiny set of gloves, gown and mask for his bear. The men who were well enough played noughts-and-crosses and hangman with him. Those who were more seriously ill got their friends to bring him chocolate and comics and other presents. There were so many gifts that Sarah would sneak them out when Matthew wasn't looking and send them to school for Tom and Adrian. I worried about the boys touching the gifts, so I wiped them with Dettol when no-one was looking. I could smell its bitterness on my hands when I got home.

Every time I went, I took a sticky iced bun in a paper bag.

There was a fight going on in my head. These men and their friends were sinners. They had the disease. They were guilty. But they loved my boy.

My beautiful godson wasn't a sinner. Not that kind. He was innocent. But he had the same disease.

If AIDS really was God's wrath, how could Matthew get so ill? And if my church – any church – believed that, how could I keep my faith?

I watched Matthew, and many of the kind young men around him, slip away. Resolving the fight in my head – that took time and conversations with gentle and wise people of many faiths and none. I met a wonderful man called Dudley Cave who created the Lesbian and Gay Bereavement Project. He explained how the Unitarians supported lesbians and gay men. And rather than losing my faith, it became stronger. I felt like I'd come home.

I left my job as a teacher and trained as a Unitarian minister. I spent a lot of time visiting the ward where Matthew had died and supporting the families of the men and boys there.

I carried out a funeral every week, sometimes more. There were iced buns, with a bright red cherry on top, at every wake. And when people asked, sometimes I would explain why.

21

Caro: An innocent victim

I think it was sheer boredom that made me swap my Observer with that woman's Sunday Express. It was the hottest day of the summer, and the air vents were pumping out even hotter air. The points failure was making an already tedious train journey even more tedious. My British Rail sandwich was somehow both soggy and dry. And I'd forgotten whether I'd ordered tea or coffee, and whichever it was, it was grim. So, by that point I was desperate.

Just inside the front page, there was an article that said children were 'being handed over to homosexual couples... despite expert advice that the youngsters may grow up to become sexually deviant themselves'. Ouch. That hurt. Sunday Express Woman caught my eye, and I gave her a wan smile. I think she was suspicious of my haircut. The only grown-up thing to do at that point was hide, so I plugged myself into my Sony Walkman and dozed off to Tracey Chapman.

Jane and I really wanted to foster, but we'd watched lesbian friends be turned down as potentials again and again. Clearly, they had been looking far too sexually deviant. Or had suspicious haircuts. So, I hatched a plan. We would have to de-dyke the house and hide who we were from the powers-that-be.

We started by clearing out the dumping ground that was the spare room to be our foster human's bedroom, and then making up the dining room as Jane's bedroom. So what if we had to eat our dinner off our knees, Jane was now officially my lodger. The visits and inspections and meetings started. And my devious plan worked. We had hidden the fact that we were a homosexual couple, and they would have no choice but to hand over children to us.

Our first foster baby was a baptism by fire. He arrived at midnight, screaming and red-faced, a tiny mite wrapped in a policewoman's jumper. He was inconsolable, and we only realised many years later that he probably had foetal alcohol syndrome. We looked after him for a week until they found a member of the family who would take him in, and I slept for fourteen hours straight after he left.

We then went into a flurry of short-term placements, some just 24 or 48 hours, a few as long as a couple of months. They were mostly babies, but we had an eleven-year-old girl as respite care when her foster carer had to go into hospital. She was sweet and sad and quiet and scared, and we had to reassure her constantly that her beloved foster mum would be fine and would be back to pick her up. Her face when her foster mum came to the door was just magical. I wanted to remember them all and so I started a book of sketches to capture their beautiful faces and their names.

And then we got Hannah. She was three months old. I think by then the social worker had worked out that Jane wasn't really my lodger, but decided that she wouldn't ask, and we wouldn't tell.

Hannah's mum was in hospital with AIDS, and they didn't expect her to come out. Those days it wasn't clear whether and how HIV could be passed onto babies, but it didn't take any of us long to realise that Hannah was ill. These days the antiretrovirals would have given her an adulthood, but she came to us too early for that.

Hannah was quiet, but she had a sparkle in her eyes and a truly dirty laugh like an East End landlady. She was her own person and was determined that we knew it. While we had the gut feeling that we weren't going to have her for long, we decided that we were going to make that 'not long' as much fun as possible, both for her and for us. She brought us so much joy, our little Hannah Banana, and she got a sketchbook all of her own.

She was only fourteen months old when she died. I remember someone calling her an innocent victim, and it took me a while to work out why that made me so angry. And then I realised. I'd lost too many people to HIV and AIDS to accept the 'innocent' and 'guilty' labels. They were just all victims of a virus that didn't care who it infected.

Jane and I were planning a break after Hannah died, and then the social worker knocked on the door.

Since the 1980s, we have fostered just under a hundred children, some for a few hours, some for years. Some sick, some healthy. Some with HIV. Tiny babies, stampeding toddlers, and an utterly adorable eight-year-old who arrived with one change of clothes and Frederick Bear.

She left us last year to go off to university, loaded with many suitcases and a threadbare Fred Bear. Laughing that we had to at least warn her if there was going to be a waif and stray in her bed when she came home for Christmas.

Because we're not done yet. There's still space on the sketchbook shelf.

22

Yvonne: The best lovers are good with their hands

I learned to sign almost before I learned to speak.

My mum was born Deaf and signs, and my dad is hearing but learned sign when he met my mum. It must have been love – he's certainly never made the effort to speak any other languages. To cut a long story short – I grew up bilingual.

When I was at secondary school I got bullied because I had the mum who made funny noises when she tried to talk and who spoke using sign language. They would mouth things silently at me, wave their hands around, make howling noises. I hate to admit it now, but I asked her not to come to school anymore. She didn't tell my dad; she just made excuses not to go when I was in a play or a concert. When dad found out, he was furious. We had the biggest row we had ever had, my mum, my dad and I, all the more intense because it was silent and in sign. What made it worse for me was how kind my mum was about it. How understanding. I had no idea how badly she had been bullied too.

They talked to the teachers at school, who set up a sign language class as an after-school club. No pun intended, but that was almost unheard of back then in the 1970s. I made new friends, and they would come home for tea and practise sign with mum and me over Findus Crispy Pancakes, baked beans and white sliced bread. One extra advantage – sign was so much better than passing notes in class.

It probably didn't surprise anyone when I trained as an BSL interpreter and teacher. I got my first job in the 1980s in a signing Deaf school.

I was eating lunch in my classroom, working on a lesson plan on Shakespeare, when the school secretary bustled in – she was a tiny bundle of energy who never seemed to stop moving. There was a call for me from the hospital. She must have seen me go white, so she said it was nothing to worry about, it was just about BSL interpreting.

It was Sister Josephine from the infectious diseases ward in the local hospital asking me if I would come in and talk to a patient. His name was James and that she not only wanted to communicate to him about his care because he was terrified, but she also wanted him not to feel so alone. She was such a kind woman.

I had no idea what to expect when I got there. I knew about AIDS – well, as much as anyone did. Sister Josephine took me into her office to prepare me for what I might see, but nothing really could.

James was afraid. He was also angry. And really very ill. As I walked over to his bed, you could see all of this on his face. I was afraid too, but as soon as I started signing his face lit up, and I felt myself relax. I started by talking to him about how he felt, and he just didn't want to stop.

He talked about his hearing parents who had been persuaded that a boarding school that used speech rather than sign was the only way that he could ever lead a normal life in a speaking and hearing world. We'd learned about these places at teacher training college. The ones that believed teaching children to sign would stop them learning to speak, and that sign was a primitive form of communication and not a full language. I'd just come away from an incredible performance that combined music and dance and sign, which was as far from primitive as it was possible to be.

These schools would punish the children for signing and force them to learn to lip-read. Lip-reading is great, but not perfect, as I found out in an exercise where we had to put in earplugs and see what we could follow in a video. People turned away, covered their faces, or shouted. The worst was the man with the really huge Father Christmas beard and moustache. I didn't think I would get anything in my stocking that year.

James told me that he was given heavy and uncomfortable hearing aids to wear, and made to sit through hours of speech therapy. Copying the teacher's mouth shapes and breathing patterns. Trying to make a piece of tissue paper or a flame move as he practised P and B sounds. The faces he made telling me about this made me laugh and I felt awful. He sat straight-faced for a moment and then smiled for the first time that day. All of this, of course, took up the time where he should have been getting an education, and he left school barely able to read and write.

He told me about his first boyfriend, Gary, watching carefully to see if I would be shocked. When he saw I wasn't, he relaxed. Gary had secretly taught him to sign, and it gave him a window into a world where he could communicate. He found joy with Gary, and he said that he could finally live.

It was hard being both Deaf and gay, he said – for some reason he couldn't understand, people couldn't seem to see that you could be both at once. And that some people thought that it made you all wrong in two totally different ways. He got really animated when he started telling me about finding other Deaf gay men at the Triangle Club when he moved to Manchester, and that was where he discovered GSV – Gay Sign Variation. I'd never heard of it, and he told me that it had started as a secret language for Deaf gay men, like hearing gay men used Polari. He showed me the signs – they were theatrical and visual, full of campness, flair and joy. It was good to hear him laugh.

He said that GSV was where he found his voice. And where he learned that the best lovers are good with their hands. I got the giggles at that, and one of the nurses had to come over to check that I was okay.

Even though James had found his tribe, he never really heard much about HIV and AIDS. His literacy levels were low, which wasn't uncommon in profoundly Deaf people at the time. And there was no sexual health provision for Deaf gay men. The only aids he knew about were hearing aids, and HIV was just a meaningless collection of letters. He didn't feel right, and he went along to the GP, where they did some blood tests. When he went back a few weeks later, the heavily bearded doctor didn't have an interpreter with him and couldn't sign. So, all James picked up was what the doctor wrote down on a piece of paper – H I V plus. Plus, he thought – positive – that means the results are good. So he left, reassured.

They wrote to him, to ask him to come back. By the time he got someone to read the letter for him, the appointment had passed, and he felt fine.

Until one day, he didn't. He collapsed in the street. A passer-by called an ambulance.

Here he was, in hospital, surrounded by people who were oh so kind, but who couldn't communicate with him to explain why he was there. And who couldn't contact his friends.

I had to break the news to him. To explain what HIV was. To tell him that it wasn't positive like 'I'm feeling really positive.' It was positive like: 'I'm sorry, you've got 'it' – the 'it' that no-one has explained to you. The one that's a life sentence.'

He gave me his friend Nicolas's address, and I went along to see him. Nicolas had been so scared because it seemed like James had just gone missing. Disappeared. It really hadn't occurred to me how easily that could happen, even for someone who was hearing, and how terrifying it could be for someone who was Deaf. I took Nicolas to see James, and after that there was a steady stream of people from the Deaf community visiting, both gay and straight. Sister Josephine was so happy she hugged me.

I called in to the hospital most days on my way home from work, to see how he was and translate for the nursing staff. A couple of the nurses even started to come along to my BSL evening classes.

The school secretary called me out of class, about a month after that first call. James had died, with one of the nurses from my class at his bedside.

I persuaded our Head to include HIV/AIDS in the school's sex education curriculum. Section 28 made it harder, but we managed. I became known as a safe person for the pupils who were trying to understand who they were – at first undercover because of the law, and later openly with a group that met after school.

I'll never forget James because meeting him changed how I teach.

I wish he'd known.

23

Hilda: It was only a little thing

It was only a little thing.

He lived below me, on the third floor. We would talk in the hallways. He'd help carry my shopping up the stairs. I'd feed his fish and collect his post when he went away. He called me Grandma and I called him a cheeky little sod. We were somewhere between acquaintances and friends. Fre-quaintance? Semi-friend?

I'd heard from another neighbour, Joan, that his family had stopped speaking to him. Thrown him out. She told me he was in hospital – a few days being looked after at the new London Lighthouse. A rest cure, my mother would have called it.

I called in to feed his fish. The flat wasn't messy but you could tell he'd left in a hurry. Plates in the sink. Mugs on the side.

I did the washing up. Wiped down the surfaces. Threw out the milk that had gone off. Ran the Hoover round. Took his sheets down with me to the launderette and gave them a good hot wash. Left a little bunch of ox-eye daisies in a jam jar – they grew on the old bomb site behind the new supermarket – on the kitchen table along with his post.

A few days later, there was a knock on the door and a little bunch of roses on the mat, with a note saying, 'Thank you – I know it was you.'

It was only a little thing I did. But, you know. He does call me Grandma.

24

Deirdre: Being a friend

They asked me to be Alan's friend. It's a strange question when you are a grown-up, to be asked to be someone's friend, but you see, the buddy service told me that Alan had AIDS and he was feeling lonely. Buddy is such a funny word – it sounds American, and I've never been further than the Isle of Wight.

Well, anyway, my sister volunteered for the service with her daughter, and they asked me to help out. And I said yes - I've not got much else to do these days, now I'm on my own. So, Alan lived on his own too, and his family were at the other end of the country. Sylvia – she's my sister - said that they didn't even know that he was ill, and he couldn't tell them. I couldn't imagine not being able to talk to my family about something like that. Not everyone has a good sister like my Sylvia, I suppose.

Back to what I was saying. I'm sorry, I do wander round the houses these days. Alan had been having a rough time since his diagnosis. Someone had put an envelope of dog – shall we say doo-doo – through his door, and someone else wrote awful things on his car. I can't even say what they wrote.

I didn't really expect us to have much in common – I'm old and I can't get out of the house much, and he's young and used to parties – but we ended up talking every week on the phone. He told me about music and his friends, and I talked about my garden. He said to me how much he loved gardens and though he didn't have one now, he told me all about helping his mum plant and weed when he was little. I think he missed the garden almost as much as he missed his mum.

I liked talking to Alan. I know I was supposed to be helping him not to be lonely, but I think he helped me just as much.

25

Marla: Tea and whisky and striped blankets

The first time I worked for a gay couple – well, I wasn't quite sure what to expect. I'd never met gay men before.

Most people I cleaned for, I never saw. Well, that's not quite true. I met them, we checked each other over. I got a key and instructions. After that, it was money left next to the toaster, and I watched their lives unfold through a haze of hot water, the pine smell of Flash, and a can of Ajax.

The single man who had a woman's toothbrush appear suddenly next to the bathroom sink. And then over the next few weeks there was make-up by the mirror in the hall and a dressing gown on the back of the bedroom door. Then it all disappeared overnight, and the copies of Playboy re-emerged under the bed.

The young marrieds who worked long hours and had busy lives. They left notes for each other on the fridge. A chapter-by-chapter story scribbled in blue Biro of appointments for date nights, reminders for shopping, slow-burn arguments, and then quick-fire joyous making up.

The artist who said I was allowed go anywhere in the house except his studio. The kitchen noticeboard was full of gallery details, invitations to exhibition opening nights, and pictures of him and an older man. Sometimes he would burst into the kitchen and show me something beautiful that he had created, and one day I found him weeping silently over a letter telling him his artist mentor had died.

The busy working mum who would leave me apologies for the mess, along with a snack, sometimes home-made. I loved her house the best – it was full of untidiness and joy and life and love and a big sleeping orange cat on the sofa who barely blinked an eye as I vacuumed around him.

As I said, I wasn't sure what to expect with Philip and William. But it wasn't really any different to the other couples I cleaned for. They shared a bed and didn't always make it after they got up. Left cereal bowls in the sink and toothpaste splattered on the mirror. Put notes next to the toaster with my envelope of money, asking me to tidy the fridge and take home anything that might spoil, as they would be away for a couple of weeks. I got to try wonderful food, flavours new to me. Hummus. Avocados. Sushi and sashimi. Indian vegetarian food, and seafood in fragrant Thai sauces. Nut loaf from Cranks.

I mean – yes – there were magazines I'd never seen before and pictures of naked men on the walls, but I'd seen posters of naked women in the single man's flat, and to be honest – I liked the Mapplethorpes better than the Playboy centrefolds.

Philip worked in a bank and William was a dancer. Theirs was a townhouse – narrow, on three floors, with a small, neat garden. Pale paintwork, lots of art and beautiful furniture. There were clippings from magazines framed on the wall: interviews with William, pictures of their beautiful and tiny garden, stills and reviews from William's shows. Interviews with him. Photographs of the two of them. William was tall, lean, slight, muscular. Philip was squarer – more of a rugby player's build. Not as tall. Handsome. You wouldn't have thought that he was gay. Well, I wouldn't. But then, what did I know?

I let myself in one afternoon and heard a sound from Philip's office, a neat small room full of books. He called out for me to ignore him. He was taking the day off ill, and I should pretend that he wasn't there, and just clean as usual. He had a hacking cough, but it was November and there was a lot of it about. He was at home a lot over the next few weeks, and the cough didn't get any better, but he brushed it off. Nothing to see.

They asked me to help out with their Christmas party – setting up, handing round little bits of food on elegant plates, cleaning up afterwards. Philip was looking thin and tired, and explained it away as the remnants of flu. But I noticed that he slipped upstairs early, which seemed unlike him. As the last few people left, I heard someone say something about Auntie Ada coming to call. It didn't mean anything to me. I just saw the worried look on William's face.

The next time I went over to clean, just before Christmas Day, it all fell into place. William and Philip sat me down in their beautiful living room and told me that Philip had AIDS, and that they understood if I didn't want to clean for them anymore. I didn't know what to say. I was sad and scared and I'm ashamed to say that I ran away. Slammed the door. Went home and ran a bath so hot it almost scalded me. Scrubbed myself from head to foot with Lifebuoy soap – the red one that smells of carbolic – until my skin stung.

I didn't sleep that night. Or the next. New Year passed in a blur, and I still didn't really know what to do. And then, almost without realising, I found myself on Philip and William's doorstep one Saturday. I had just raised my hand to the knocker when William opened the door, a black bin bag in his hand.

I tried to explain, to say that I was sorry, but he just ushered me down the side of the house, into the garden. He disappeared into the kitchen and came back out, a few minutes later, with mugs of steaming hot tea laced with whisky and armfuls of brightly striped, soft blankets. We sat in the sunny, cold January morning and he poured his heart out to me. Philip was dying in front of his eyes. Fading away. He was falling apart. The house was… well… He just looked at me. I finished my tea, got my cleaning caddy out of my tiny Ford Fiesta, and set to work.

There was shit and piss and vomit on the bathroom floor. William had done his best to clean it up, but every time he stepped away from the bedside, Philip tried to get out of bed and fell. There were piles of soiled bedding in the hallway. The kitchen was full of washing up and the fridge still held Christmas party leftovers.

I cleaned all day. Hung load after load of clean sheets out in the cold bright sun. Emptied the fridge and the bins. Got some money from William and drove to the shops. Made chicken soup the way my grandmother did, and fed it, spoon by spoon to Philip while William dozed on the sofa.

I bathed when I got home, but the water wasn't scalding, and the soap came from Marseilles and was scented with roses – a gift from Philip to wash away the smell of bleach and disinfectant.

I went in two or three times a week – as often as I could between jobs, really – and I took in food for both of them. It wasn't sashimi or Thai seafood; it was the soups and stews that my grandmother had taught me to make when my mother was out cleaning.

The word got around that I was willing to work for people with HIV. Sometimes there would be family and friends caring for the young men. Sometimes I would be the only visitor. Sometimes I would cook and shop. Sometimes I would be the one who called the ambulance.

I worked invisibly, cleaning dead men's flats around friends looking lost and talking in small groups, or hiding away things from weeping mothers. Comforting grieving parents who had only just discovered that their son was gay and now they had a funeral to arrange.

I went to funerals with drag queens and Methodists. Salvationists and fetishists. Gay men in leather and quiet weeping parents in tweed. One of those was Philip's.

I see William sometimes, even though I'm now retired. We drink tea laced with whisky in his still-beautiful garden and talk about Philip, and about love.

26

Bridgit: Dental dams and safer sex

When I saw the *Killer in the Village* documentary in 1983, I didn't see what AIDS – I don't even think it was called that then – had to do with women. And as things went on, there wasn't a lot to change my mind. Any discussions about sex just talked about men who have sex with men and anal sex, and then after a while, penis-in-vagina sex, when they finally accepted that it wasn't just the gays. The straights could get it too. What a shock.

There was the occasional discussion about dental dams, but really – have you even seen one? I saw *Aliens* in 1986 at the cinema and yelled, 'Oh, dear Lord, it's a dam!' when the Facehugger appeared. My girlfriend Julia lost it, and we got escorted out by a shocked usher. We did try one, but Julia just wouldn't stop sniggering. She told me that it was like being tickled through a carrier bag. I suggested clingfilm, and she laughed until her stomach hurt. So, we decided not to bother with that bit.

Other than this, there really wasn't anything telling lesbians how to stay safe. We felt abandoned. The lack of information left us angry, and a bit scared. We were even accused of 'virus envy' by some gay men. Sometimes it felt like we were disappearing.

After what seemed like ages, a few guides emerged that talked about woman-on-woman sex. And you could spot the ones written by lesbians for lesbians a mile off! These talked to us like adults about what was safe, what may be safe, and what was risky. Explained that the risk was low but not non-existent. Told us to be open and honest and set limits, and then left us to make our own choices.

There's historically been animosity between some gay men and lesbians. I still remember the shout of 'I can smell fish!' when I walked into a gay bar. Because of this, some women were reluctant to help out because they didn't truly believe that the men would have been there if the tables had been turned, but there were others who did so much, from caring and cleaning to fundraising and activism. In the US, the San Diego Blood Sisters got women to donate blood in a time of great need, and Kristen Ries and Maggie Snyder quietly cared for patients in Salt Lake City.

While I'm not one to look for silver linings in clouds – some clouds just bring storms – the crisis did bring lesbians and gay men together. I did hear that the L comes first in LGBT+ because of the care we gave in the 80s. I don't know whether it's true, but it's a nice thought.

27

Pat: Excluded

If this was a film, I'd say the first time I saw her, birds suddenly appeared, or the sun rose in her eyes. But it's not. And they didn't. And we were only six. But I did know that I wanted to be around her. She wore the nicest dresses, and had the blondest curls tied up with a purple ribbon. I wore shorts and plimsolls with holes in, and I had permanently scabby knees. Straight brown hair escaping from a plait. And National Health glasses with the bendy wire bits round your ears, and sometimes the bit of plaster because I'd broken them. Again. My mother was constantly so proud.

We were best friends. When we were at primary school, we had fish fingers and baked beans round each other's houses. When we were teenagers, we sat on my bed and listened to the chart countdowns on a Tuesday on Radio 1 on my crackly transistor radio. We played the three LPs that we owned between us over and over again until my parents yelled up the stairs. We went roller skating at the leisure centre on a Saturday morning. She talked about the boys she liked, and took the mick out of me about never having been kissed. She tried to get me into a skirt and make-up for the school disco. I did it once and changed half-way through into jeans and a T shirt because I just couldn't stand how it felt. But she also came with me when I went to the barbers for my first short haircut and let me cry on her shoulder when the girls at school called me a lesbo in the changing rooms. She listened and understood when I told her that I liked girls. And she kept it secret.

Sally discovered drama at school and got the leading roles every time. She joined the local youth drama group. Maybe I was biased, but I thought she acted everyone else off the stage. Back in my bedroom, we spent hours going through her lines, talking about the roles, discussing her character's motivation, bitching about the director and making plans for Sally's glittering future. I was almost as excited as she was when she got into drama school in London.

I'd followed her to the youth theatre, where I fell in love with the dust and paint smells and darkness behind the scenes. I discovered that I was actually really good at it too. Making props. Painting scenery. Stage management. Sometimes prompting too, but that made me way too anxious. After hours of arguments with my dad about 'doing a proper subject', I got a place at a college up north to do theatre studies.

I'd learned to hate the word 'lesbian' when I was at school – I heard it too many times yelled across the playground or whispered in the toilets. It felt like something wrong. Or dirty. It certainly didn't feel like what I was. And then one day in the refectory I overheard a couple of other students – women – talking about dykes. At last, I had a word that fitted as snugly as my favourite old Docs. They caught me staring and I blushed and glared at my nut loaf and lumpy mashed potato. When I looked up, they'd gone, but there was a flyer on the table in front of me. Lesbian and Gay Soc October Social. And there it was. My whole new beginning.

Sally and I lost touch somewhere around my second year – trains were expensive, coach travel sucked, and we were at different ends of the country. We wrote for a while but that tailed off. I missed her so much.

A year or so after I graduated, I was an ASM at a small and grubby theatre in London. It was the first day of on-stage rehearsals for a new play, and I was halfway up a ladder fixing a hole in a flat. I was most probably covered in dust, with God-only-knows-what in my hair and a screwdriver tucked into my paint-stained dungarees. The director was shouting. As usual. But over the hammering and bawling I heard a familiar voice. I looked down and there she was, sitting cross-legged on the floor, talking to someone I assumed was going to be the leading man. She wore a baggy purple silk shirt and black waistcoat, tight stonewashed jeans and gorgeous black suede pixie boots. Her hair was piled up on her head in a messy bun. She looked – perfect.

She saw me and grinned, a surprised and dazzling smile. I blushed and melted inside.

She stood up in one movement, almost boneless, something I remembered from those nights listening to music. She started across, but then the director called everyone to the stage. He told the cast that I was the go-to person for pretty much everything and there wasn't much I couldn't fix. He dismissed me. I carted the ladder off stage, almost walking into the wall as I couldn't take my eyes off her.

I watched the rehearsal from the wings. Even though they were only blocking out the first few scenes, Sally acted everyone off the stage. As she always did.

We spent that evening in my favourite bar drinking bad white wine and swapping stories of the past few years. As always, she did most of the talking and I did most of the listening. As we hugged when the bar shut, she gave me a drunken kiss.

I lay awake all night revisiting that kiss. I told myself it was a 'luvvie' kiss. A drunken kiss. That it meant nothing. That she had a boyfriend – the leading man, as it turned out – and he was wonderful. Good-looking. Charming. Talented. Everything a woman could want. But I couldn't stop thinking about her lips on mine. Her body heat under her thin silk shirt. What her skin would feel like. Taste like. What the fold of her neck would smell like. I finally slept but my dreams were tangled.

I saw her every day in the theatre. Every night after rehearsals and shows when she wasn't seeing him. Which was more often than I expected – he seemed to spend a lot of time 'networking' – but I didn't care. I would take every moment I could get.

One night when rehearsals over-ran, I slept on the floor of her room in her tiny, cheap and draughty shared flat. In the early hours of the morning, she drew me into her bed, saying that she was cold. I settled to sleep as far away from her as possible, but she pulled me close and took my face in her hands. Leaned in and kissed me, and her skin and her taste and her smell were everything I hoped for. I moved in with her the next day, with all my scanty belongings, and those first few weeks were the happiest I had ever been. But then the entire company went down with flu. Somehow, I avoided it, but I became everyone's mother, handing out sympathy, Vocalzones, Lemsip, tissues, and bad jokes about Fishermen's Friends.

We limped through the final week of the play. Sally just couldn't shake the bug off. She was feverish, achy and sick, and she missed a period. We got one of the new pregnancy tests, and she peed on the piece of paper, and I put it into three different pots. Those were the longest 30 minutes ever but no blue. So, it was all exhaustion and post-play lows.

She finally shook the flu off, and her periods came back, but they were heavy and painful. Those days she would curl on the sofa, pale and shaky, with my old teddy bear hot water bottle and a stack of blankets. When she didn't have a period, she had thrush or pelvic pain, headaches or night sweats. Within just months of us getting together I was her nursemaid, not her lover.

She began to lose weight, and I got scared. Even more scared when I heard that her leading man was in hospital. They said skin cancer, but the word around the theatres was that his 'networking' had been with a young man. Or young men.

The day she passed out on the floor and didn't know me when she woke up, I called an ambulance. They took her to Guy's Hospital, into the women's ward. It took them an age to diagnose her, despite everything I said about her actor, because nice young white girls weren't any of the four Hs –heroin users, homosexuals, haemophiliacs, and Haitians. It wasn't until I saw her in the hospital bed that I realised how much weight she had lost. I know she felt that I was sending her away. Abandoning her. But I couldn't manage any more on my own. I hated myself for that for a long time, but I was so young and so afraid.

Finally, they moved her into a side room in the infectious diseases ward. The nurses stared at me when I visited – I don't know whether it was my dungarees and boots or that she was the only woman there. When she went into intensive care, they wouldn't let me in. I even tried to dress up as straight in a frock and shoes borrowed from the wardrobe mistress. I felt as I had at the school disco, but it didn't make any difference. I wasn't family. And anyway, her mother had told them to keep me away. The nurses were kind, but what could they do?

I never saw Sally again.

I was excluded from her disease, because she caught it from a man. Excluded from the hospital, because her mother somehow saw it all as my fault. Excluded from the funeral by a furious family member who hissed that I had no right to be there. Excluded from our home, because she hadn't left a will or any instructions. Why would she? She was so young. She didn't expect to die. And finally excluded from all my memories because her sister took everything – Sally's and mine – and burned it the day they found out that she had AIDS.

The theatre became my home. Literally. Until the wardrobe mistress found me asleep on the tatty sofa in the greenroom. She took me into her home and surrounded me with children and dogs and love and warmth and laughter until my heart healed.

The theatre has always been my family and my life. Every play I write has a character called Sally. Every stage set I create has a splash of purple somewhere. And any time I direct, I remember everything she taught me about the art of acting.

Thank you, Sally, for what you gave to me.

Wish you were here to see it.

28

Naomi: No weddings, three funerals

The first person I knew with AIDS got ill really fast. My girlfriend Maura and I stood outside the hospital where Duncan was being treated for pneumonia, reassuring each other that we couldn't catch it by touching people, hugging them, or even being in the same room.

I walked in and kissed him, and he said, with his best sarcastic grin, 'You've never kissed me before – what are you trying to prove?'

Duncan was wearing gorgeous burgundy silk pyjamas, and his boyfriend had set up a bar in his room. There was gin and tonic, a bottle of Beaujolais, champagne, a board of French cheeses and a bowl of kumquats. I'd never seen a kumquat before, and when I tried to peel one, Duncan giggled himself silly.

A few weeks later, we got a call to go to the London Lighthouse. We were told that Duncan had stopped eating and drinking, and this could be our last chance to see him. We knew it was going to be hard, but nothing prepared me for it. The skin was stretched thin and yellow over his skull, and I could count every rib through his satin robe. He was only 23 but he looked like an old man. It was really shocking. We stayed as long as we could, trying to act normally. We left in silence, completely traumatised.

We were in our twenties. People our age didn't die in hospices.

Maura and I went out for the most extravagant dinner that we could afford and raised a glass to Duncan, convinced that we would never see him again.

After a night on intravenous fluids, Duncan got up, rolled his drip stand to the day room and had a cigarette, a bowl of soup and a cup of tea. A few days later, we got another call. Duncan was knocking at death's door again. Maura and I had another extravagant meal. I get dark under stress, and I remember saying to her that we couldn't afford for him to keep on not dying.

Duncan's funeral was at the Lighthouse. We wanted a pint beforehand but didn't know the area. We walked into the first place we saw with blacked-out windows – that was how you usually spotted a gay bar in those days – and ended up in a strip joint. The beer was expensive, but we really needed it. We ignored all the funny looks and smiled at the startled girl on the grubby stage.

When we arrived at the funeral, we were given a glass of whisky and told to drink it before we walked in, as 'you're really going to need it.' The casket was open, and Duncan had refused to have his body 'prepared' – he wanted everyone to know what

AIDS really looked like. He appeared to have died mid-scream. Beside the coffin there was a picture of how beautiful he had looked at 20. Everyone filing past swore or shrieked. It was just... horrific.

We were given tea and Battenburg cake. The funeral directors walked in silently, picked up the coffin, and walked out. No speeches. No graveside moment. Just silence.

The next funeral was worlds apart. Ian, an old friend from college, developed AIDS, and when he started to get really ill, he invited his friends to morning coffees and afternoon teas at the best hotels in London. He put it all on his credit card, announcing, 'the debt dies with me, darlings.' He ate ice cream – the only thing he could stomach – and bought everyone roses. The funeral was packed full of beautiful young people. It was standing room only and I hovered at the back in my best suit and tie. The most glorious trans woman, a vision in shoulder pads and heels and scarlet lip gloss, swept up to me. She whispered, 'Oh darling, I didn't know that there were any butch dykes left. Escort me to the front.'

The crowds parted like the Red Sea for Moses, and I found myself in the front row amidst the glitz and glamour and famous names and gold credit cards.

The next funeral was of my friend Nicholas's ex. He was a nurse and had fallen in love with a patient with AIDS. He deliberately infected himself with the patient's blood – he wanted them to die together. The church was full of nurses in capes and hats and friends wearing red ribbons, the first time I'd seen those. Nicholas sat resolutely in the front row, even after he was told that it was reserved for family. They all squeezed into the pew on the other side, leaving him there alone amongst the flowers and the torch songs. We followed the coffin out of the church, sobbing like children, sweaty, emotional and dishevelled.

I sat in the pub with Nicholas and his mum in silence, double gin and tonics in front of each of us. Nicholas broke the quiet by saying that his ex's parents had told everyone he'd died of leukaemia.

After that I stopped going to funerals. I couldn't do it anymore.

29

Audrey: We've both grown old

One of the first people I knew with AIDS – the first I knew well, anyway – has just turned 75. When he was diagnosed in late 1984, we didn't think he would see the year out, let alone a quarter of the way into the next century. And anyway, we were young, and the thought of 75 was impossibly old and impossibly far away. Now, we've both grown old.

Greg was my flatmate. We'd met when we taught in the same school, and living together was camouflage for both of us – a lesbian and a gay man in what might have looked like a lavender marriage, but without the piece of paper or the pretence of sharing the same bed.

I taught physical education. Yes, I know, butch lesbian with a hockey stick, but in my defence, I really like hockey. Greg taught physics. Did that rattle your expectations? Admit it, you expected English or RE, didn't you?

In a lot of ways, we were like any other couple. Conversations over who fed the cat – we started leaving notes, as said cat was so good at claiming no one fed him ever. Arguments over washing up. We spent evenings settled on the sofa watching telly. Saturday afternoons listening to music. Me painting protest signs for Lesbians and Gays Support the Miners. Him ironing his vest and jeans on a folded towel on the coffee table, getting ready to go to Islington to see his mate's band, Cardinal Sin and the Abominations. So, maybe not totally like any other couple.

One morning he showed me the mark on his chest. It looked like a purple birthmark. It wasn't his first symptom, apparently, but it was the first he'd admitted to me. I persuaded him to go to the STI clinic, and they told him there. He started on AZT, a nucleoside reverse transcriptase inhibitor – and he said the side effects made it feel like he had been nuked. He stopped sleeping and his head pounded, and he said he wasn't sure whether he'd rather be ill. The rumours started to spread about him after a parent spotted him out one night. Funny how no-one asked the parent why he was in that particular pub, but there you go. The school pretended they were getting rid of him because he was too ill to work, and Section 28 and side-effects meant that he couldn't face fighting it.

We limped through. I kept my head down at school after Greg 'left', and got a new job as soon as I could. We rubbed along together with hospital admissions and daily cocktails of the handful of drugs that were available. More and more like an old married couple every day.

Then the protease inhibitors arrived. These felt like miracle drugs – they made him feel so much better. As he responded, his doctors decided to push his treatment harder to get the virus down even further. This is where it got complicated. At one point he was talking 17 pills a day at different times, each with its own food restrictions and side effects. There was a schedule for his drugs on the fridge more complicated than my school timetable and the cleaning rota put together.

Me? I was just there, being his 'wife' and looking after him. Making the right meals at the right times. Reminding him what drugs to take and when. Driving him to hospital when he got ill. Dealing with the psychological fallout of the treatment and talking him down when it all got too much. Like the day I found him looking at himself in the mirror and sobbing, his favourite, perfectly ironed jeans just hanging off him because the nukes and the PIs meant that he had lost fat from his legs and his bum.

Everyone was there for him. They were all wonderful. But it felt like there was no-one there for me. We'd both had to deal with so much change, and one day I broke. Perhaps I had relaxed because I realised how much better he was feeling. Perhaps I was simply just tired. But one of my colleagues found me weeping wordlessly in the showers after school, fully dressed and soaked to the skin.

I moved out while he was away. Left him a letter. Explained that I needed space. Time. A rest.

I started a new life somewhere far away.

I still feel guilty, all these years on. Sometimes I wonder about reaching out. Now that we have both grown old. But I don't think I will.

Happy birthday, Greg.

30

Kirsty: Jacob's story - it's not over yet

In creating this collection, I have watched the HIV/AIDS pandemic unfold from the first case to the present day. From a diagnosis of almost certain death to something that people live alongside.

The first antiretroviral against HIV was approved in 1987. Since then, the advent of better and safer drugs now means that people who live with HIV can achieve an undetectable level of virus and cannot transmit HIV to sexual partners (U = U or Undetectable = Untransmittable). Antiretrovirals reduce the transmission rate of HIV from mothers to babies, and PrEP (pre-exposure prophylaxis) means that people can protect themselves from infection.

However, the HIV pandemic is not over yet. According to the World Health Organization, over 600,000 people die every year from the virus, and in 2022, 1.3 million people were newly infected with HIV. There are a lot of factors behind this. Some people don't know that they are HIV-positive, so they don't seek treatment or avoid spreading the virus. Others cannot access the healthcare they need, or face fear and stigma that stops them coming forward. Sadly, some deny the existence of HIV, or do not accept the link between HIV and AIDS, a viewpoint that has re-emerged alongside COVID-19 conspiracy theories. This denialism doesn't affect just the individuals; it has an impact on the people around them as well.

You know it's not going to be a good day when it starts with someone shouting. Even more so when they are shouting at you.

Jacob's parents weren't happy. And that was a bit of an understatement.

Jacob was 16. He was bright and articulate. Confident. Good looking. When I met him, he'd just passed nine GCSEs, all at 8 or 9, and was planning to do science at A level. On top of this, he was apparently good at football, but I'm afraid I was no judge of that. He certainly loved talking about it. He was what my mum would have called an all-round good egg.

Jacob was HIV-positive. We will never know when he was infected with the virus, but it may have been at birth. If this was the case, he was fortunate enough to be one of the rare individuals whose disease hadn't progressed quickly. Though not fortunate enough, as he had started to show symptoms of AIDS at 15, the year before I first met him. His doctor wanted to start him on antiretroviral treatments to stop things getting worse, and he agreed. But there's a 'but'. I only get involved when there's a 'but'. His parents refused treatment.

The NHS took his parents to court, and it then went to the High Court. That's where I came in. I was his guardian in the courts, and I worked with his legal team on his behalf.

In the hearing, Jacob spoke directly to the High Court judge, an older woman whose stern look, contradicted by grey eyes with a twinkle, reminded me of my favourite English teacher. Even though he was overawed by the grand and unfamiliar environment, Jacob stood up straight and tall and spoke clearly and confidently. He loved his parents. He respected their views. But he was starting to feel ill. He told the judge how sick his father had become without treatment and that his mother was getting ill too. He told her that he wanted to get better. He wanted to go to university and become an engineer like his father. And he really wanted to play football again.

I met with his parents to see if there was any room for discussion. Jacob's parents were from Eswatini – it used to be called Swaziland. It's a small and beautiful country in the south of Africa, but unfortunately, it's best known as the HIV capital of the world. His dad – I'll call him Sipho, but obviously none of the names are real – was an engineer. He came over to the UK to study for a master's and stayed to work. He was a talented engineer and an intelligent man. Charming like his son. Articulate and loving. Wanting the best for his family. Someone who, in any other context, I would have liked as a friend. However, he was also someone who knew his own mind and wouldn't change his views easily.

His wife, Thembie, came over to the UK with him, bringing their daughter and son. Thembie was quiet and soft-spoken. Looked to her husband for his lead. Nodded along with everything he said. But I knew she was clever too and was studying for a degree in African History.

Despite both being HIV-positive and showing signs of illness, he and his wife didn't believe that HIV causes AIDS. Sipho told me that many people who tested positive did not go on to develop AIDS, and many more people with AIDS had never been HIV-positive. I asked if he was saying that HIV doesn't exist.

'Of course not. It exists,' he said, as if explaining something really obvious to a small child, 'but it's harmless, like a cold virus.'

I asked him where he got this idea from, and he told me that it was all about the science. While he was clearly trying hard to remain calm, underneath it he was getting irritated with me. He had a bulging folder in his hand. He slammed it down on the desk and sheets of printed paper spilled out across the shiny surface. I picked one up, a printout from one of the more inflammatory HIV denialist sites. I put it down again, and Sipho pointed to a paragraph, highlighted in harsh yellow.

'There are thousands of papers published on HIV, and not one has ever truly proved that the virus causes the disease. More and more scientists are questioning the theory that HIV causes AIDS, even those who were previously convinced. And that's all it ever was. A theory.'

This is where he started to shout, jabbing his finger at me.

'AIDS in Africa is a Western relabelling of unsanitary conditions, parasitic infections, malnutrition, and diseases like malaria and tuberculosis. Your government could have helped us in Africa by providing food and treating these diseases. But instead, you gave us the so-called anti-AIDS drugs, and we stayed weak and sick. AIDS in Europe is caused by your degenerate lifestyles – recreational drugs and alcohol and too much sex. We came here for a better life for our son, but we were wrong. Jacob didn't have AIDS while he was in Africa – he only got it when he got here.'

He looked at the wedding photo on my desk – the picture of my wife and I – and scowled. Clearly my queerness was just another example of the AIDS-causing miasma of degeneracy that had somehow infected Jacob.

My struggle to stay calm and professional fought with the part of me that wanted to stand up and shout. I thought about the beige folder in my bag that held the literature that could refute all his points, but I knew it would be futile to argue with him. Instead, I showed them details I'd found about a local youth group for HIV-positive teenagers, and told them that Jacob's medical team had a specialist clinic treating young people.

I also let them know that Jacob had been allocated a local authority social worker, a young black man with family roots in southern Africa, as well as a huge love of football and links to the local team. I knew Gabriel well, and we'd talked for hours about Jacob, his parents, and the need to build a trusting relationship. Gabriel would be able to link Jacob up with the youth group, where he could meet teenagers with similar experiences. Gabriel had also met with the medical team, where they had explained Jacob's condition and answered all of his questions.

As they left, Sipho angrily screwed up the notes I'd given him and left them on the desk. I sighed. While it went against the grain, I knew I had to tell the court that they had no role here. It was frustrating, but driving a wedge between Jacob and his parents would only be counterproductive. We needed to wait before taking the next step.

And then everything changed.

I got a call from Thembie that Sipho had been rushed to hospital, and that it wasn't looking good. Also, she and Jacob weren't well. I went round to the house, where I found Jacob asleep on the sofa, under a pile of colourful throws, his older sister Mary at his side. She was 18, and the only member of the family who had escaped infection.

I went upstairs to where Thembie lay in bed. She had lost so much weight since the last time I saw her, and her voice was husky. She beckoned me over and told me that she had just heard Sipho had died, and that she knew she was really ill. She went quiet for a moment and then started to whisper. I leaned in. There were tears running down her exhausted face. She told me that she would not stop Jacob getting treatment. I thanked her. I think she was already asleep before I got to the door.

Over the next few days, Jacob's social worker and I met with Jacob, his medical team and his sister, who had agreed to be his legal guardian and carer if (or sadly when) his mother died. He began treatment straight away and joined the youth group where he made some amazing, funny, football-loving friends.

The court concluded the case, and with it, my formal connections with Jacob and his family. Gabriel and I kept in touch for a while – he continued to support Jacob and Mary. Jacob responded well to the treatment. After a year out of school he went back to begin his A levels.

He began to look at university websites. And he started playing football again.

Acknowledgements

A huge thank you to all the lovely people (too many to mention) who have helped me out by reading, editing, critiquing and providing encouragement and performance space.

An even bigger thank you to the amazing women who have trusted me with their stories, including Cath, Jude, June, Linda, Maggie, Michele, Nicola and Sue.

Thank you also to the incredible people at Switchboard, the Bishopsgate Institute and Reconnecting Rainbows Press. A donation from every copy sold will go to Switchboard to support their work as the national LGBTQIA+ support line

And finally, the biggest thank you to my wonderful wife Dee for your love, support and encouragement, and for your amazing cover art.

If any of these stories have resonated with you, please consider supporting LGBTQIA+ and AIDS charities. My favourites are:

Switchboard (www.switchboard.lgbt)
Stonewall (www.stonewall.org.uk)
Terrence Higgins Trust (www.tht.org.uk)
Positive East (www.positiveeast.org.uk).

About the Author

Suzanne Elvidge's writing crosses science and the arts, covering fact, fiction and the blurry spaces in between. She writes fiction about unheard women's voices based on interviews, news stories, historical events and the overheard. Her writing about healthcare, medicine and research has been published in New Scientist, Scientific American, and Nature. She lives on the North Yorkshire coast with her illustrator wife and sundry dogs and cats, and she seems to think swimming in the North Sea in winter is A Good Thing.

Photo: Paul Armstrong / The Artistic Lens

BOLD, BEAUTIFUL, BOUNDARY-BREAKING LITERATURE FROM QUEER STORYTELLERS

POETRY

Tubelines   by Kestral Gaian   978-1-9158930-9-3
A map of movement, memory, and meaning across fifty poems.

Counterweights   by Kestral Gaian   978-1-8383425-3-1
A collection of poems about the duality of human nature.

Trans*(Verse) I   edited by Ash Brockwell   978-1-787234-09-3

Trans*(Verse) II   edited by Ash Brockwell   978-1-8383425-0-0
Two collections of poems and lyrics by transgender and non-binary writers from around the world.

The Boy Behind The Wall   by Dalton Harrison   978-1-8383425-2-4
Poems of loss, imprisonment, and freedom.

Emotional Literacy   by Ash Brockwell   978-1-8383425-6-2
Poems of love, loss, reverse culture shock, and surviving depression.

Potry   by Jenet La Lecheur   978-1-915893-06-2
A collection of delightfully stoned poems.

QUEER HISTORY

Twenty-Eight edited by Kestral Gaian 978-1-8383425-5-5

Stories from people who grew up under the shadow of the UK's "Don't Say Gay" laws of the 1980s, 1990s, and early 2000s.

PLAYS

Diana: The Untold and Untrue Story by Linus Karp 978-1-915893-05-5

Do you know the story of Princess Diana? Probably. But do you know *this* story of Princess Diana? We very much doubt it.

YOUNG ADULT

Hidden Lives by Kestral Gaian 978-1-8383425-8-6

A story of loss, friendship, and staying true to who you are against all odds.

Twisted Roots by A. G. Parker 978-1-915893-03-1

A dark contemporary fantasy, which weaves together the stories of magic, redemption, and compassion.

CHILDREN'S

Spidercat by Alex Francis 978-1-915893-02-4

Spider isn't an ordinary cat, and there's nothing wrong with that!

www.ingramcontent.com/pod-product-compliance
Lightning Source LLC
Chambersburg PA
CBHW052048070526
44584CB00017B/2096